DESIRED TRACK

DESIRED TRACK

The Tragic Flight of KAL 007

VOLUME TWO: THE EVIDENCE

James Gollin
&
Robert Allardyce

AMERICAN VISION PUBLISHING - Findlay, Ohio

INTRODUCTION

This second volume of our analysis supplies the vital statistics on which the narrative account in the first volume is based. These include the courses, latitude/longitude positions at key times, airspeeds, distances flown, winds, fuel burn and, perhaps most significant, FAA-certified returns from the radars at Kenai and King Salmon Air Force bases that tracked KE007's flight across Alaska.

This volume also contains our detailed discussions of such issues of special concern as Inertial Navigation Systems, the ETP and the Buffer Zone.

Events have long outrun the theory that a 10° error in inserting KE007's longitude at Anchorage International Airport was responsible for the jumbo jet's "innocent" deviation from course. But we feel that our refutations of this theory in both its forms should stand. They testify to the zeal with which self-styled experts, some of them knowingly, have promoted wrong explanations of the flight.

Some readers will find the weight of the numbers and the press of technical detail tedious if not positively numbing. Perhaps very few will be curious enough to plot the courses and positions and times and speeds, to see if these data bear out our account. But the essence of objective inquiry is to put forth the evidence as well as the conclusion. The truth of KE007's flight is in the details. Here they are.

Robert W. Allardyce
James Gollin
August, 1995

The desired track (DSRT) was designed to give us the true track to fly between two waypoints. If we started on track and always flew the desired track, we would stay on track.

Trans World Airlines 747 Flight Handbook (1985), p. 19

It is error alone which needs the support of government. Truth can stand by itself.

Thomas Jefferson

TABLE OF CONTENTS

INTRODUCTION

KE007'S COURSES
GEOGRAPHIC COORDINATES OF
WAYPOINTS AND KEY LOCATIONS
AND RELATED TIME AND DISTANCE DATA
A. COURSE BASED ON INITIAL CALCULATIONS
B. COURSE BASED ON INTELLIGENCE DATA

Waypoint #	Fix	COURSE A Coordinates	COURSE B Coordinates
o	Anchorage Airport	N61°10.5'/W149°59.6'	----
ONE	Anchorage VOR	N61°09.1'/W150°12.3'	----
	1st radar 1302.53Z	N61°12'53.8"/ W150°14'11.4"	----
o	HDG mode 1304.26Z	N61°12'40.4"/ W150°28'31.9"	----
o	Triple Mix 1309.52Z	N61°11'27.3"/ W151°30'06.5"	----
o	Abeam CRN	N61°12.1'/W155°33.0'	----
o	Bethel VOR	N60°47.1'/W161°49.3'	----
o	Abeam BET	N61°59.7'/W161°49.3'	----
TWO	Beyond BET	N60°46.6'/W165°00.0' dist. from R-20 course = 93.1nm	N60°37.9'/W165°45.0' dist. from R-20 course = 119.7nm
THREE	Abeam NABIE	N60°22.2'/W172°28.6' dist. from R-20 course = 74.1nm	N60°36.2'/W172°39.5'
o	Into BZ[1]	N60°20.6'/W174°00.0'	N59°40.5'/W175°55.0'
o	Update ETA NEEVA	N60°11.8'/W175°38.3'	
o	Exit BZ	N59°42.0'/W180°00.0'	N59°02.7'/W180°00.0'

1

FOUR	Abeam NEEVA[2]	N57°35.0'/E168°36.0'	N57°13.2'/E171°33.0'
FIVE	1551Z[3]	N58°24.8'/E167°17.3'	N58°03.0'/E170°15.0'
SIX	into KAM[4]	N55°03.1'/E161°59.0'	N55°03.0'/E162°05.0'
o	Exit KAM[5]	N52°45.6'/E156°12.0'	N53°00.0'/E156°10.0'
SEVEN	Abeam NIPPI[6]	N52°32.6'/E155°43.0'	
EIGHT	1st turn 1802Z	N47°07.5'/E145°52.3'	----
o	2nd turn 1807Z	N47°27.7'/E144°55.5'	----
o	JSDA[7] 1812Z	N47°40.0'/E143°45.0'	----
o	Over SAKH[8]	N47°14.2'/E143°01.3'	----
o	Missile strikes[9]	N46°32.6'/E141°51.4'	----
o	Moneron Island	N46°17.0'/E141°15.0'	----
o	Search center	N46°35.0'/E141°20.0'	----
o	Main wreckage	N46°33'32"/ E141°19'41"	----

NOTES

1. BZ = Buffer Zone.

2. 1542Z, start of 320° leg.

3. Start of 220° leg

4. KAM = Kamchatka Peninsula

5. Distance across Kamchatka, 268nm.

6. Distance from exit point = 21.9nm, distance from NIPPI = 218.1nm.

7. JSDA = Japan Self Defense Agency Radar. Distance to Sakhalin entry = 39.2nm.

8. SAKH = Sakhalin Island

9. Distance from point of entry = 63.3nm.

KE007'S FLIGHT
GEOGRAPHIC COORDINATES OF
ADDITIONAL KEY LOCATIONS

DESCRIPTION OF FIX	COORDINATES
St. Paul Island (SPY)	N57°09.5'/W170°13.6'
Track A at abeam NABIE	N60°22.2'/W172°28.6'
Track B at abeam NABIE	N60°36.2'/W172°39.5'
Track Y at abeam NABIE	N60°26.8'/W172°40.0'
Intelligence track at abeam NABIE	N60°28.6'/W172°39.0'

TIMES, DISTANCES AND LOCATIONS ON
220° APPROACH TO KAMCHATKA

Times and Distances	Track Y locations	Intelligence track locations
1551Z (0nm)	N58°24.8'/E167°17.3'	N58°03.0'/E170°15.0'
1600Z (65nm)	N57°35.0'/E168°58.6'	N57°29.6'/E168°30.5'
1608Z (130nm)	N56°45.2'/E164°41.7'	N56°58.8'/E167°00.6'
1620Z (209nm)	N55°44.7'/E163°10.5'	N56°10.7'/E164°50.2'
1630Z 287.8nm (Track Y landfall)	N55°03.1'/E161°59.0'	----
1635Z (Intelligence Track landfall)	----	N55°03.0'/E162°05.0'
1706Z (exit)	N52°45.6'/E156°12.0'	N53°00.0'/E156°10.0'

WAYPOINTS ON
J501/R20
ANCHORAGE, ALASKA - SEOUL, SOUTH KOREA

WAYPOINT NUMBER[1]	WAYPOINT NAME (FIX)	COORDINATES
o[2]	Cairn Mountain	N61°06.0'/W155°33.0'
ONE	Bethel (BET) VOR	N60°47.1'/W161°49.3'
TWO	NABIE	N59°18.0'/W171°45.4'
o	Nukks	N57°15.1'/E179°44.3'
THREE	NEEVA	N54°40.7'/E172°11.8'
o	Ninno	N52°21.5'/E165°22.8'
FOUR	NIPPI	N49°41.9'/E159°19.3'
o	Nytim	N46°11.9'/E153°00.5'
FIVE	NOKKA	N42°23.3'/E147°28.8'
SIX	NOHO	N40°25.0'/E145°00.0'
SEVEN	NANAC	N38°54.2'/E143°13.9'
EIGHT	INKFISH	N39°30.0'/E142°45.0'
NINE	MATSUSHIMA	N38°21.5'/E141°09.3'
TEN	NIIGATA	N37°57.1'/E139°06.7'

NOTES

1. On occasion, it appears that KAL flight crews used the location of the Anchorage VOR as Waypoint One. This, of course, would change the numbering downline.

2. o = non-reporting waypoint.

SPEEDS FILED (FLIGHT-PLAN SPEEDS) AND SPEEDS FLOWN: KE007 AND KE015

LEG OF FLIGHT	FILED	FLOWN
Cairn-BET		
KE007	M.840	M.874*[1]
KE015	M.840	M.872
BET-NABIE		
KE007	M.840	M.836*
KE015	M.840	M.842
NABIE-NEEVA		
KE007	M.840	M.900/M.876*
KE015	M.840	M.854
NEEVA-NIPPI		
KE007	M.840	M.869*
KE015	M.840	M.866
NIPPI-NOKKA		
KE007	M.840	M.938[2]/M.934[3]
KE015	M.840	M.907
NOKKA-NOHO KE015	M.840	M.861

NOTES

1. * = speed for KE007's actual course.

2. Speed computed between point of exit over Kamchatka and point of 1802Z turn toward Sakhalin.

3. Speed computed between point of exit over Kamchatka and point of 1812Z JSDA radar fix.

James Gollin & Robert Allardyce

WIND COMPONENTS AND TEMPERATURES
REPORTED BY KE007 AND KE015

LOCATION AND ALTITUDE	WIND COMPONENT	TEMPERATURE
BETHEL		
KE007[1] 31,000	295/25	-49C
KE015 33,000	310/27	-56C
NABIE		
KE007 31,000	250/60	-49C
KE007 (Buffer Zone update)	250/65	-49C
KE015 33,000	245/50	-56C
NEEVA		
KE007 31,000	270/55	-48C
KE015 33,000	260/45	-52C
Kamchatka		
KE007 33,000	280/62[2]	??
NIPPI		
KE007 33,000	320/45	-49C
KE015 35,000	355/70	-52C
NOKKA		
KE015 37,000	310/65	-48C
Sakhalin		
KE007 33,000	260/56	??

NOTES
1. KE007's reports based on conditions at reporting points along actual course.

2. Winds here and over Sakhalin based on NOAA meteorological data and ICAO windfield data.

8

SYNOPSIS OF DISTANCES:
FLIGHTPLAN (R-20)
A. COURSE BASED ON INITIAL CALCULATIONS
B. COURSE BASED ON INTELLIGENCE DATA
SLANT-RANGE DISTANCES BETWEEN KE007'S WAYPOINTS
ON COURSES (A) AND (B) AND R-20

BETWEEN		DISTANCES ALONG COURSES[1]		SLANT-RANGE DISTANCES TO R-20 WAYPOINTS[2]	
	Flight Plan[3]	Course A	Course B	Course A	Course B
ANC/BET	346.0	346.2	346.2	---	---
BET/NABIE	312.0	318.0	315.3	313.2	313.2
NABIE/NEEVA	593.0	601.9	654.3[4]	595.1	593.7
NEEVA/NIPPI	560.0	534.4	529.5	568.4	575.3
NIPPI/NOKKA	664.0	666.3	658.6	700.3	698.2

NOTES

1. Distances measured in nautical miles (nm).

2. Slant-range distances are those between KE007's positions on Courses (A) and (B) and the upcoming R-20 waypoints at the times position reports were made.

3. Distances on KE007's computerized flight plan.

4. Distance comprises distance from abeam NABIE (N60°36.2'/W172°39.5') to point of 1542Z northwesterly turn (N57°13.2'/E171°33.0'), or 529.3nm, plus distance from there to point of 1551Z intelligence fix (N58°03.0'/E170°15.0'), or 65.0nm, plus distance along southwesterly track toward Kamchatka to point abeam NEEVA (N57°37.0'/E168°33.0'), or 60.0nm.

9

KE007'S GREAT CIRCLE COURSE ACROSS ALASKA; ANALYSIS OF KENAI AND KING SALMON RADAR RETURNS

As far as we know, the first person to suggest publicly that KE007, although deviating from course very soon after its departure from Anchorage, was being guided by properly functioning INS's was Richard Witkin of *The New York Times*. Writing on November 17, 1983, Witkin quoted "aviation experts" and J. Lynn Helms of the FAA as suggesting that a misprogramming of otherwise working "onboard computers" might have caused the deviation.

Later, simulation flights conducted by ICAO investigators with the cooperation of Boeing Aviation and Litton Industries produced two possible explanations for the deviation, one of them the "ten-degree error" theory first reported by Witkin. Each scenario was predicated on the assumption that KE007's INS's were working properly.[1]

ICAO investigators also had access to radar returns from Kenai and King Salmon Air Force bases targeting both KE007 and KE015 on the morning of August 31, 1983. These were used to show that KE007 began its deviation about ten minutes after departure, passed about six nautical miles north of track at Sparrevohn and about 12 nautical miles north of Bethel. The investigators, however, drew no further conclusions from the radar data.[2]

Harold H. Ewing, a 747 captain for Flying Tiger Air Lines, was the first person to realize that the radar data describe a smooth Great Circle course from a point somewhat west of Anchorage across the Alaska mainland and out over the Bering Sea. His analysis of the data was inaccurate; and his use of his findings was tendentious in that it reflected an absolute determination to promote an "innocent" explanation of KE007's excursion into Soviet airspace.[3] But Ewing's enlightening discovery prompted us to make our own analysis of the radar data. Our findings are detailed in Volume I, Chapter 2. Here we describe our methodology and supply comparative figures.

The methodology is simple. It consists of using the navigational computer to generate model Great Circle course segments (GCc's) and comparing these with KE007's geographic locations as shown in the FAA-certified radar returns every 23 to 24 seconds for the first half-hour of the flight, then every 60 seconds for the next eighteen minutes, twenty-five seconds.

The comparison is made by means of a computerized LOTOL (Longitude to Latitude) program. This analyzes GCc's by displaying, for every degree of longitude the course crosses, the exact latitude at the point of crossing. The more closely the latitudes and longitudes of the computerized GCc correspond with those of the radar returns, the more certain it is that KE007's actual course was in fact a Great Circle course -- preplanned, electronically computed and smoothly flown under the control of the INS-autopilot complex.

The GCc we determined, after experimentation, to be the correct one has as "root" the coordinates of the Anchorage VOR (N61°09.1'/W150°12.3') and, as a second and defining location, a point at the edge of the Bering Sea (N60°46.6'/W165°00.0').[4]

As the LOTOL test results indicate, the match between the radar returns and the Great Circle course we generated is extremely exact. It should be pointed out, however, that KE007 did not join this course until 1312.11Z. Until 1309.29Z, in fact, it was being flown in HDG (heading) mode. At 1309.29Z, its INS's were engaged and the aircraft was placed on a joining or "capturing" track, itself a Great Circle course segment. The capture of the main GCc took place at 1312.11Z.

NOTES

1. *ICAO Report* (1983), p. 3.

2. *Ibid.*, pp. 38-39.

3. For our view of this explanation, see "Ewing Addendum."

4. Our method of ascertaining this location is given in *Narrative*, p.40.

Desired Track Vol II: The Evidence

LOTOL TEST

Great Circle Course: N61°09.1'/W150°12.3' to N60°46.6'/W165°00.0'

Time of radar fix	Latitude	Longitude	Hdg.(True/Mag.) & Deviation
1302.53Z	N61°12.9'	W150°14.2'	---
GC comparison	N61°09.2'	W150°14.2'	3.7nm N.
1303.17Z	N61°12.8'	W150°17.6'	266.5/241.4
GCc	N61°09.2'	W150°17.6'	3.6nm N.
1303.40Z	N61°12.8'	W150°21.3'	270.0/245.0
GCc	N61°09.4'	W150°21.3'	3.4nm N.
1304.03Z	N61°12.8'	W150°22.9'	270.0/245.0
GCc	N61°09.4'	W150°22.9'	3.4nm N.
1304.26Z	N61°12.7'	W150°28.5'	266.9/241.9
GCc (Bgn HDG)	N61°09.5'	W150°28.5'	3.2nm N.
1304.50Z	N61°12.6'	W150°32.3'	266.9/241.
GCc	N61°09.6'	W150°32.3'	3.0nm N.
1305.13Z	N61°12.5'	W150°35.8'	266.6/241.6
GCc (5,000')	N61°09.7'	W150°35.8'	2.8nm N.
1305.25Z	N61°12.5'	W150°38.0'	270.0/245.0
GCc	N61°09.8'	W150°38.0'	2.7nm N.
1305.59Z	N61°12.3'	W150°43.6'	265.8/241.8
GCc	N61°09.9'	W150°43.6'	2.4nm N.
1306.23Z	N61°12.3'	W150°47.9'	270.0/246.0
GCc	N61°10.0'	W150°47.9'	2.3nm N.
1306.46Z	N61°12.1'	W150°52.2'	264.5/240.5
GCc	N61°10.1'	W150°52.2'	2.0nm N.
1307.09Z	N61°12.0'	W150°56.8'	267.4/243.4
GCc (Adj HDG)	N61°10.3'	W150°56.8'	1.7nm N.
1307.32Z	N61°11.9'	W151°01.1'	267.3/243.3
GCc	N61°10.3'	W151°01.1'	1.5nm N.

1307.56Z	N61°11.8′	W151°06.3′	267.8/243.8
GCc	N61°10.5′	W151°06.3′	1.3nm N.
1308.19Z	N61°11.7′	W151°10.7′	267.3/243.3
GCc	N61°10.6′	W151°10.7′	1.1nm N.
1308.42Z	N61°11.7′	W151°15.9′	270.0/246.0
GCc	N61°10.7′	W151°15.9′	1.0nm N.
1309.05Z	N61°10.8′	W151°20.6′	265.0/241.0
GCc	N61°10.9′	W151°20.6′	0.7nm N.
1309.29Z	N61°11.6′	W151°25.2′	272.6/248.8
GCc	N61°10.9′	W151°25.2′	0.7nm N.
1309.52Z	N61°11.1′	W151°30.1′	267.6/243.6
GCc	N61°11.1′	W151°30.1′	.4nm N.
Joining GCc	N61°11.5′	W151°30.1′	<0>
1310.15Z	N61°11.4′	W151°35.2′	267.7/243.7
GCc	N61°11.0′	W151°35.2′	.4nm N
Joining GCc	N61°11.5′	W151°35.2′	<0.1>
1310.38Z	N61°11.5′	W151°39.8′	272.6/248.6
GCc	N61°11.1′	W151°39.8′	.4nm N.
Joining GCc	N61°11.5′	W151°39.8′	<0>
1311.01Z	N61°11.5′	W151°44.8′	270.0/246.0
GCc	N61°11.2′	W151°44.8′	.3nm N.
Joining GCc	N61°11.5′	W151°44.8′	<0>
1311.25Z	N61°11.5′	W151°49.8′	270.0/246.0
GCc	N61°11.5′	W151°49.8′	0nm *[1]
Joining GCc	N61°11.5′	W151°49.8′	<0>
1311.48Z	N61°11.5′	W151°54.9′	270.0/246.0
GCc	N61°11.6′	W151°54.9′	0.1nm S.
Joining GCc	N61°11.5′	W151°54.9′	<0>
1312.11Z	N61°11.5′	W152°00.0′	270.0/246.0
GCc	N61°11.5′	W152°00.0′	0nm *
Joining GCc ends[2]	N61°11.5′	W152°00.0′	<0>
1312.34Z	N61°11.5′	W152°05.1′	
GCc	N61°11.5′	W152°05.1′	0nm *
1312.58Z	N61°11.6′	W152°10.3′	
GCc	N61°11.6′	W152°10.3′	0nm *

Desired Track Vol II: The Evidence

1313.21Z	N61°11.7′	W152°15.4′	
GCc	N61°11,7′	W152°15.4′	0nm *
1313.44Z	N61°11.6′	W152°20.7′	
GCc	N61°11.8′	W152°20.7′	0.2nm S. **[3]
1314.08Z	N61°11.7′	W152°25.8′	
GCc	N61°11.8′	W152°25.8′	0.1nm S. ***[4]
1314.31Z	N61°11.8′	W152°31.1′	
GCc	N61°11.9′	W152°31.1′	0.1nm S. ***
1314.54Z	N61°11.9′	W152°36.4′	
GCc	N61°11.9′	W152°36.4′	0nm *
1315.18Z	N61°11.8′	W152°42.0′	
GCc	N61°12.0′	W152°42.0′	0.2nm S. ***
1315.41Z	N61°11.9′	W152°47.5′	
GCc	N61°12.1′	W152°47.5′	0.2nm S. ***
1316.16Z	N61°12.2′	W152°55.4′	
GCc	N61°12.1′	W152°55.4′	0.1nm N. ***
1316.39Z	N61°12.0′	W153°01.4′	
GCc	N61°12.2′	W153°01.4′	0.2nm S. ***
1317.02Z	N61°12.2′	W153°06.6′	
GCc	N61°12.2′	W153°06.6′	0nm *
1317.25Z	N61°12.1′	W153°12.6′	
GCc	N61°12.3′	W153°12.6′	0.2nm S. ***
1317.49Z	N61°12.3′	W153°18.1′	
GCc	N61°12.3′	W153°18.1′	0nm *
1318.12Z	N61°12.3′	W153°23.9′	
GCc	N61°12.3′	W153°23.9′	0nm *
1318.35Z	N61°12.3′	W153°29.6′	
GCc	N61°12.3′	W153°29.6′	0nm *
1318.59Z	N61°11.4′	W153°36.3′	
GCc	N61°12.4′	W153°36.3′	1.0nm S. **
1319.22Z	N61°12.5′	W153°41.2′	
GCc	N61°12.4′	W153°41.2′	0.1nm N. ***

1319.45Z	N61°12.2'	W153°47.4'	
GCc	N61°12.4'	W153°47.4'	0.2nm S. ***
1320.09Z	N61°12.3'	W153°53.1'	
GCc	N61°12.4'	W152°53.1'	0.1nm S. ***
1320.32Z	N61°12.5'	W153°59.1'	
GCc	N61°12.4'	W153°59.1'	0.1nm N. ***
1320.55Z	N61°12.2'	W154°05.2'	
GCc	N61°12.4'	W154°05.2'	0.2nm S. ***
1321.18Z	N61°12.8'	W154°10.9'	
GCc	N61°12.4'	W154°10.9'	0.4nm N. **
1321.42Z	N61°12.8'	W154°16.9'	
GCc	N61°12.4'	W154°16.9'	0.4nm N. **
1322.05Z	N61°12.7'	W154°23.1'	
GCc	N61°12.4'	W154°23.1'	0.3nm N. ***
1322.28Z	N61°12.5'	W154°29.3'	
GCc	N61°12.4'	W154°29.3'	0.1nm N. ***
1322.52Z	N61°12.5'	W154°35.6'	
GCc	N61°12.6'	W154°35.6'	0.1nm S. ***
1323.15Z	N61°12.5'	W154°41.8'	
GCc	N61°12.3'	W154°41.8'	0.2nm N. ***
1323.38Z	N61°12.9'	W154°47.6'	
GCc	N61°12.3'	W154°47.6'	0.6 nm N. **
1324.02Z	N61°12.5'	W154°54.3'	
GCc	N61°12.3'	W154°54.3'	0.2nm N. ***
1324.39Z	N61°12.6'	W155°06.6'	
GCc	N61°12.2'	W155°06.6'	0.4nm N. ***
1325.12Z	N61°13.2'	W166°12.5'	
GCc	N61°12.1'	W166°12.5'	1.1nm N. **
1325.35Z	N61°12.5'	W155°19.0'	
GCc	N61°12.1'	W155°19.0'	0.4nm N. ***
1325.58Z	N61°12.0'	W155°25.7'	
GCc	N61°12.0'	W155°25.7'	0nm *

Desired Track Vol II: The Evidence

1326.22Z	N61°12.1′	W155°31.8′	
GCc (CRN)	N61°12.0′	W155°31.8′	0.1nm N. **
1326.45Z	N61°11.7′	W155°38.4′	
GCc	N61°11.9′	W155°38.4′	0.2nm S. **
1327.09Z	N61°12.0′	W155°44.3′	
GCc	N61°11.8′	W155°44.3′	0.2nm N. ***
1327.32Z	N61°11.6′	W155°50.9′	
GCc	N61°11.7′	W155°50.9′	0.1nm S. **
1327.55Z	N61°12.0′	W155°57.0′	
GCc	N61°11.6′	W155°57.0′	0,4nm N. **
1328.18Z	N61°11.8′	W156°03.2′	
GCc	N61°11.6′	W156°03.2′	0.2nm N. ***
1328.42Z	N61°11.7′	W156°09.6′	
GCc	N61°11.5′	W156°09.6′	0.2nm N. ***
1329.05Z	N61°11.7′	W156°15.9′	
GCc	N61°11.4′	W156°15.9′	0.3nm N. **
1329.28Z	N61°12.3′	W156°22.0′	
GCc	N61°11.3′	W156°22.0′	1.0nm N. **
1330.30Z	N61°11.9′	W156°41.6′	
GCc (Begin AKN)	N61°10.9′	W156°41.6′	1.0nm N.***
1331.18Z	N61°11.7′	W156°55.1′	
GCc	N61°10.6′	W156°55.1′	1.1nm N. **
1332.18Z	N61°11.2′	W157°11.4′	
GCc	N61°10.3′	W157°11.4′	1.1nm N. **
1333.18Z	N61°10.9′	W157°28.8′	
GCc	N61°09.9′	W157°28.8′	1.0nm N. **
1334.18Z	N61°10.6′	W157°44.5′	
GCc	N61°09.5′	W157°44.5′	1.1nm N.**
1335.17Z	N61°10.2′	W158°01.0′	
GCc	N61°09.0′	W158°01.0′	1.2nm N.**
1336.29Z	N61°09.4′	W158°22.4′	
GCc	N61°08.3′	W158°22.4′	1.1nm N. ***

1337.17Z	N61°08.9'	W158°35.7'	
GCc	N61°07.9'	W158°35.7'	1.0nm N. ***
1338.18Z	N61°08.6'	W158°51.5'	
GCc	N61°07.4'	W158°51.5'	1.2nm N. ***
1339.17Z	N61°08.9'	W158°35.5'	
GCc	N61°07.9'	W158°35.5'	1.0nm N. ***
1340.17Z	N61°07.2'	W159°24.1'	
GCc	N61°06.1'	W159°24.1'	1.1nm N. **
1341.17Z	N61°05.9'	W159°42.1'	
GCc	N61°05.4'	W159°42.1'	0.5nm N. **
1342.18Z	N61°05.3'	W159°58.4'	
GCc	N61°04.7'	W159°58.4'	0.6nm N. **
1343.17Z	N61°04.7'	W160°14.2'	
GCc	N61°04.0'	W160°14.2'	0.7nm N. **
1344.17Z	N61°03.7'	W160°30.4'	
GCc	N61°03.3'	W160°30.4'	0.4nm N. **
1345.17Z	N61°02.7'	W160°46.9'	
GCc	N61°02.5'	W160°46.9'	0.2nm N. **
1346.17Z	N61°01.5'	W161°03.8'	
GCc	N61°01.6'	W161°03.8'	0.1nm N. **
1347.17Z	N61°01.1'	W161°19.1'	
GCc	N61°00.8'	W161°19.1'	0.3nm N. **
1347.53Z	N61°00.9'	W161°29.4'	
GCc (final return)	N61°00.2'	W161°29.4'	0.7nm N. **

NOTES

1. * = on course

2. KE007 captured its desired track at 1312.11Z.

3. ** = effect of changed upper wind velocity.

4. *** = correcting for effects of wind shifts.

"HOW-GOES-IT?" FUEL BURN ANALYSIS

The most usual form of "How-Goes-It?" chart affords a flight crew a continuous comparison between the fuel poundage the flight plan indicates should be aboard and the actual poundage at the given moment. Any significant drop below the preplanned fuel requirement is thus immediately noticeable.

Our approach, however, reverses the norm, charting not fuel remaining but fuel consumed during the course of KE007's flight. On the graph we created (to save space, it is not reproduced here), one line represents fuel consumption at the rate reflected in the 747's computerized flight plan. A second line, almost superimposed on the first, depicts flight-plan consumption adjusted *by us* for such actualities as lesser fuel burnoff during taxiing and lighter-than-anticipated headwind between the top of KE007's climb to its cruising altitude (TOC) and Bethel. Our purpose was to show the extent to which actual fuel consumption would have varied from predicted (flight-plan) consumption had KE007's flight crew truly flown its approved J501/R-20 route on the morning of August 31, 1983.

The upper line of our graph represents fuel use based on the direct or relayed position reports of KE007. It is obvious at a glance that KE007's flight crew, starting with its NABIE position report, announced that it had consumed roughly 9,000 pounds more fuel than the flight plan called for. At NABIE, copilot Sohn reported that fuel remaining was "two one niner decimal zero," or 219,000 pounds. If we are correct that Captain Chun had loaded an additional 10,000 pounds of fuel aboard KE007 at Anchorage, making the total fuel load 263,700 pounds (see Volume I, pp. 2-6), Sohn's report might mean that the aircraft had burned 44,700 pounds between Anchorage and

Bethel, an amount more than one-third greater than the 33,324 pounds the fuel burn should have been that night. Alternatively, it might mean that Sohn was covering up the fact of the added fuel by basing his report on a falsely low 253,700-pound ramp fuel figure. Or it could mean that Sohn had caught a Chun arithmetic error in midflight and was basing his reports on a 253,700-pound figure that was not false at all but correct.

Beyond NABIE, reported fuel burn and adjusted consumption remain roughly similar. One discrepancy, however, does show up. KE007 reported arriving at waypoint NEEVA nearly nine minutes later than its flight plan called for -- this despite a head wind that was slackening. The implication is that it slowed its air speed to below the flight plan speed of M.840. Under normal circumstances, such a slowdown would *lower* fuel consumption. But for what was supposedly the NABIE-to-NEEVA leg of KE007's journey along R-20, copilot Sohn reported fuel usage of 39,000 pounds, whereas the flight plan called for a burn-off of 34,300 pounds. The difference is a significant 4,700 pounds. One cannot have it both ways: a slower speed and a higher-than-M.840 fuel burn. In fact, KE007 *was* flying at speeds lower than M.840 -- through the Buffer Zone and toward the Kamchatka Peninsula.

Still another fuel-use anomaly develops when one looks at the following depiction of what KE007's flight plan would have shown had its crew been conscientiously logging burnoff:

Desired Track Vol II: The Evidence

Station	Distance	Mag Course	Mag Hdg (°)	Alt (000)	Fuel Pln/Act
BET	174	2438	242	31	222.7/219.0
NABIE	312	2382	237	31	204.0/200.0
NEEVA	297	2345	235	33	169.7/161.0
NIPPI	279	2383	242	33	139.9/132.0

By the time it had supposedly reached NEEVA, roughly the halfway point on an R-20 flight to Seoul, KE007 had burned off 8,700 more pounds of fuel than its flight plan called for. Any flight crew that thought it was plodding along at M.840 would have been worried by this shortfall. But of course KE007's crew was not on R-20. And while at times KE007 was flying at speeds slower than M.840, it was hardly plodding along.

INERTIAL NAVIGATION SYSTEMS

The primary navigational devices aboard KE007 were its three Litton LTN-72R-28 Inertial Navigation System units. Indisputable evidence has long since surfaced that KE007, which very soon after takeoff began deviating from its authorized J-501/R-20 course, was nonetheless being guided by INS's in working order during most legs of its flight.

A basic understanding of the INS and how it works will help shed light on a central question of the KE007 disaster: how did KE007's flight crew, on a course steadily diverging from the course on which it was supposed to be flying, nevertheless supply the air traffic controllers on the ground with convincingly timely and authentic reports of its positions, estimated times of arrival at subsequent reporting points and other flight information?

What is an INS?

The first point to be made about the Inertial Navigation System is that it is a completely self-contained system. That is, it is capable of guiding an aircraft from place to place without reference to any external aid, either natural (e.g., the sun, the moon, the stars, a river) or manmade (a church steeple, a radio beacon, a radar signal).

In addition to guiding the aircraft, via a linkage with the autopilot which controls the rudder and other flight surfaces, the INS supplies the flight crew a continuous flow of information (it can also supply "spot" or occasional information) about the status of the flight.

Litton Industries INS's like those aboard KE007 *each* consist of three separate units. One, located in the electronics bay in the hull of the aircraft, is the Inertial Navigation Unit, a "platform" of electronic sensors. These, first of all, establish the *horizon* of the aircraft, which in turn allows the pilot to know its attitude -- the all-important matter, especially at high altitudes beyond sight of the ground, of whether it is flying level or cocking upward or downward. Secondly, the sensors register the aircraft's *movement*, no matter how tiny and no matter in which direction. This unit also houses a computer which performs the navigational computations.

The two other units of each INS are located on the flight deck. One, the Central Display Unit, is the device by which a flight crew member can enter or display navigational data: the display itself is a set of readout windows which present the ever-changing data digitally.

The control knob of the second flight deck unit, the Mode Selector Unit, allows a crew member to choose among the several different operating modes of the particular INS.

Each INS has its own independent electric power source and its own back-up battery. Each can store in its memory-banks the latitude/longitude coordinates of up to nine geographic positions, called "waypoints," forming a given course. Each can provide steering commands to the aircraft's autopilot that will guide the aircraft from waypoint to waypoint, automatically adjusting for wind.

As noted, each INS can display a wealth of en route navigational data, including the aircraft's present position and speed over the ground, the distance and time at a given speed to the next waypoint on its course, the position of all waypoints on the course and the winds on the nose and tail of the aircraft and how these affect direction and speed,

Boeing 747's and other commercial aircraft flying transoceanic routes will typically be equipped not with one but with two or three Inertial Navigation Systems. Of these, the

No. 1 or "command" INS, located at the pilot's station, and the No. 2 INS, at the copilot's, can each be linked to the autopilot to actually control the aircraft in flight. The No. 3 INS, if carried, is used by the flight engineer to navigate and to log off data for the position reports made at intervals to ground-based air traffic controllers. Often (but not always), No. 3 INS is not independently linked to the autopilot.

Although each INS is an independent unit, the three INS's can and do interact. We will discuss their interaction below.

INS navigation.

If circumstances permit, air navigators can guide their aircraft to its destination via radio beacons and other ground-based navigational aids. Or they can use the traditional compasses, chronometers and parallel rulers of dead reckoning to plot their courses. For that matter, they can get their aircraft from its point of origin to its destination via the tried-and-true method of flying from landmark to landmark along the way. Whatever method is used, the sensors and CDU of the Inertial Navigation System will supply the flow of data a navigator needs to be sure that the aircraft is on course.

But the only navigational method by which an INS will actually actuate the autopilot and *guide* the aircraft is Great Circle course (GCc) navigation based on the mathematics of spherical geometry and spherical trigonometry.

For our purposes, the most important of the spherical geometry theorems involved are: 1) any two points on the surface of a sphere can be connected by an arc which is a segment of a circumference (a Great Circle) of the sphere; and 2) this arc is the shortest distance between the two points. The INU computer uses spherical trigonometry to measure Great Circle distances, whether of ten nautical miles or a thousand, and to generate other navigational information as the aircraft moves; but a detailed explanation is beyond the scope of this addendum.

How the INS works.

To operate at all, an aircraft's INS's must be "initialized" on the ground before each flight. Electric power is switched on and the latitude/longitude coordinates of the exact spot on which the aircraft is parked are entered via keypad into the memory banks of all INS units. All subsequent flight data will be derived from this one geographical "fix."

It takes about 20 minutes for the horizon orientation to become operative and for the INS's to accept the aircraft's initial location. Once initialization is complete, the INS's are ready to navigate the aircraft.

Having thus "told" the INS's where they are, the pilot (or other flight-crew member: the practice varies from airline to airline) must then tell them where they are to go. Accordingly, he types into the memory banks of each INS the coordinates of some or all of the waypoints over which he wants his aircraft to fly en route.

This might be the appropriate place to point out that while a Great Circle segment always is the *shortest* distance between any given origin and any given destination on the face of the globe, the shortest-distance route is not always the most practical or most efficient route for aircraft to follow. Many factors, from wind and weather conditions to international politics, may recommend a route that is longer in nautical miles but briefer in terms of time -- or longer in miles and time but safer.

Certified transoceanic airways are seldom if ever single Great Circle segments stretching from origin to destination. Almost always, they are sets of waypoints spaced at more or less regular intervals for navigational efficiency and economy. As for the waypoints themselves, rarely is an oceanic waypoint an island and never is it, as some seem not to be able to grasp, an actual navigational aid, a floating signal beacon. Rather, it is no more than a geographic reference point, a dot on the map of the sea. This notwithstanding, waypoints on some routes are given names. Typically, the names of all waypoints on any one airway will have the same initial letter.

We have already pointed out that INS's can actually guide an aircraft only on Great Circle courses (GCc's). It follows that the courses between waypoints on an airway (or on any other route on which an aircraft is being guided by INS) are all Great Circle courses. Or, to put it slightly differently, *a route on which the aircraft is guided by INS, if it is not a single Great Circle course, is a sequence of linked GCc segments, each segment being the distance between one waypoint and the next.*

As noted, each INS will accept the latitude/longitude coordinates of up to nine waypoints. If there are more than nine along a given route, then at some point the flight crew will have to type the coordinates of the tenth and successive waypoints into the INS, using the "slots" of waypoints already passed.

To an INS, Waypoint Zero is the ever-changing instant location of the aircraft itself.

The fact is useful in many ways. If a pilot wants to bypass a given waypoint -- Waypoint One, for example -- he simply types into his INS the command message "Zero to Two." The INS coupled to the autopilot will immediately make any adjustment in course needed to fly the aircraft on the Great Circle course segment between its present position and Waypoint Two. Or if the pilot or navigator wants to know the distance from the aircraft's immediate location to the upcoming waypoint, and the amount of time it will take to get there, he need only quiz the INS's computer and it will instantly offer him the answers in digital format on its console.

If a pilot senses that he is off the proper track (for navigational purposes, "track" can be thought of as the noontime shadow cast on the ground by an aircraft moving with absolute accuracy from place to place), he turns the knob on his Central Display Unit to the position labeled XTK/TKE (for "Cross Track Distance/Track Angle Error"). The Cross Track Distance reading will tell him immediately, in nautical miles and tenths of a mile, how far the aircraft is to the right or the left of the correct or "desired" track. The Track Angle Error reading will tell him the number of compass degrees the aircraft must be turned, right or left, to get it back on its desired track.

Leg-switching and alert light functioning.

On an INS route along which are several waypoints, the GCc segments between waypoints are known as "legs" of the flight. To make good the GCc segment marked by a given waypoint usually requires a greater adjustment to the aircraft's track than that already demanded by the nature of its previous GCc.

If the turn needed to join the new leg were delayed until the aircraft actually overflew the waypoint, the maneuver would be abrupt enough to disturb the passengers but, given the laws of physics, not possibly exact enough to put the aircraft on its new course without overshooting and requiring a time-and-fuel-wasting correction. (At some weights and altitudes, also, the forces exerted on the aircraft's control surfaces by so sudden a turn could precipitate a high-speed stall.)

The simple solution to these difficulties is to begin the turn onto the new track before reaching the waypoint.

The "leg-switching" function of the INS permits this smoothing-out of the turn. Usually, under leg-switching, the gentler turn begins about 15 seconds before a waypoint would be reached. The roll-out, the aviation term for the emergence from the turn, occurs precisely on the new flight path. The curvature of the turn is such that the waypoint often lies slightly outside the turn's circumference.

It is important to note that the greater the upcoming course change, the earlier the leg-switching must begin for the change to be smooth, and the further the waypoint will be beyond the circumference of the turn.

It is also extremely important to know that leg-switching will take place even if the aircraft is approaching a position *abeam* the actual waypoint location. By "abeam position," we mean the position -- it can be any distance either to the left or the right of the waypoint -- where the aircraft would have to make a 90° turn to reach the waypoint.

Two minutes before the aircraft's arrival at a waypoint, under normal circumstances, an amber "alert light" blinks on. Its purpose is to inform the flight crew of the need to begin compiling the information that must be passed on to air traffic control in the impending position report.

The alert light, however, does not remain on for the full two minutes. As soon as leg-switching begins, the light goes off. The time remaining between the moment at which the light is extinguished and actual passage of the waypoint thus varies depending on the severity of the aircraft's turn. If the turn must begin well before waypoint passage to be smooth, the alert light might be illuminated for only one minute or -- in extreme circumstances -- thirty seconds or even less.

When the distance between the waypoint and an aircraft's *abeam* position is greater than about 200 nautical miles, the alert light program seems to be disrupted. Tests indicate that the light will flash on earlier than the two minutes for which it is programmed and will stay lit for only a few seconds.

Time and distance data presentation.

As noted, an aircraft's INS's offer continuous digital readouts of the time and distance remaining to the next waypoint. This intelligence is of course based on the "Waypoint Zero" or "INS" position -- where the INS, at the exact instant, determines the aircraft to be.

Immediately as leg-switching occurs and the new track is joined, the INS computers present the new time and distance readings for the next waypoint.

Triple mix and disparity functions.

Multiple INS's aboard a given aircraft are interrelated only through two systems: the "triple mix" and disparity systems.

The computer software program known as "triple mix" was developed to facilitate greater accuracy in air navigation by comparing the input/output of each INS with that or those of the others. Under normal circumstances, triple mix makes an INS consensus available to the autopilot, which will direct the course of the aircraft based on the triple mix "Waypoint Zero" or "INS" position.

Triple mix can be and often is enabled on the ground prior to takeoff, but may also be enabled at any time during flight. The flight crew types in a discrete numerical command to initiate the program. Another command must be inserted to deactivate it.

The disparity system of the LTN-72R-28 is specifically designed to safeguard navigation system integrity. On this model, if one INS "Waypoint Zero" position differs from those of the others or from the triple mix position by an amount determined by a simple formula or by 35 nautical miles, whichever is greater, the action and malfunction CDU warning annunciator light will flash, and code messages "8" and "01" will appear in a readout window, signifying "do not use INS for HSI

[Horizontal Situation Indicator] or steering" and "failed intersystem comparison test."[1]

The message can be cleared, but the erring INS must be updated or reprogrammed before it will go back on line.

Short of a 35nm disparity, a formula that takes into account the time-span of the flight will trigger the "8/01" message. The formula is $3T + 3 = D$, where T = time since initialization, D = disparity in nautical miles. Thus, the shorter the flight (actually, the shorter the time since INS initialization) the smaller the allowable disparity.

On a two-hour flight, for example, a deviating INS will have to be reprogrammed if its disparity is greater than nine (3 x 2 + 3) nautical miles.

INS functioning and the KE007 departure from course.

In our narrative (pp. 7-10, 18-21), we discuss at length the issues arising from the fact that KE007's INS's were in good operating order. In particular, we deal with the possibility that an accidental misprogramming of an otherwise properly functioning INS caused KE007 to stray off-course. In this volume (p. 33ff.), we test Harold H. Ewing's theory that the combination of an accidental misprogramming and a deliberate but erroneous reprogramming led to KE007's disastrous departure from its proper course.

And so, what remains to be discussed here are the further INS anomalies that would have led KE007's flight crew, had it been unintentionally or "innocently" off-course, to recognize the fact and take prompt corrective action.

First, consider the INS "alert light" which flashes on two minutes before a waypoint is reached. At eight nautical miles per minute (the rule-of-thumb Mach speed equivalent for M.840, KE007's required Mach speed), the INS "Distance To" display should read "16" and the "Time To" display, "2.0" minutes. As the aircraft nears the waypoint, both mileage and time will count down, though never down as far as "zero" because leg-switching will ease the aircraft onto its new track before the waypoint is reached.

KE007 passed abeam Bethel, the "gateway" waypoint of its R-20 transoceanic route, 12.6 nautical miles to the north. Had the aircraft had the Bethel waypoint coordinates in its INS's as it cruised by, at the instant the alert light signalled two minutes to go to the waypoint the "Distance To" reading would have been not 16 nautical miles but 16.9. The distance countdown would proceed -- abnormally slowly -- but it could never read less than 12 nautical miles. Further, the "Time To" reading at the instant the alert light was triggered would not have been "2.0" but something slightly more: perhaps "2.1." And it would never count down beyond about "1.5."

It could be argued (and has been) that discrepancies this small could have passed unobserved. We disagree, but we are willing to assume for the sake of the discussion that KE007's crew did not notice that the aircraft failed to overfly Bethel and did its leg-switching only about fifteen seconds shy of the waypoint.

NABIE is a different story.

By the time KE007 had reached a point abeam NABIE (the first oceanic waypoint on R-20), it was 74.1 nautical miles north of course. At the point when the alert light blinked on, the "Time To" reading would have been "2.0," but the "Distance To" reading, instead of being "16," would have been "66.9." A discrepancy this large would alarm the most complacent airmen. Also, the course change from 65nm abeam NABIE to the next R-20 waypoint, NEEVA, would certainly have been more extreme than that from NABIE itself to NEEVA. So leg-switching would have to have begun much sooner than normal, and the alert light would thus have blinked off much earlier.

When KE007 passed abeam NEEVA, it was 187.5nm north of course. At this distance, the alert light, if it switched on at all, stayed lit for only a few seconds. When the "Time To" reading was "2.0," the "Distance To" would have read, not "16," but rather "188.2."

No flight crew, however disoriented or deranged, could have overlooked these INS anomalies. Nor did KE007's crew overlook them, *because they never occurred.* The main body of our work demonstrates that KE007's actual course on the morning of August 31, 1983, was preplanned to take it further and further from R-20 and into Soviet airspace over Kamchatka and later over Sakhalin. The aircraft's INS's flew it exactly where it was meant to fly. The times of waypoint passage and of estimated arrival at the next waypoint, the winds and the temperatures the crew proffered to air traffic controllers in its position reports were all derived from INS data at KE007's actual positions. These data, although at times at variance with conditions along airway R-20, were accepted by the controllers without demur.

NOTES

1. *Pilot's Guide, LTN-72R Area Navigation System*, pp. 3-30-31, 9-1.

EWING ADDENDUM

Of the several theories advanced to provide an "innocent" explanation for KE007's deviant flight path, one of the most elaborate and most durable was that of Harold H. Ewing, a veteran pilot with extensive flight experience aboard 747's who is a captain with Flying Tiger Airlines.

Professing to be motivated by professional curiosity and concern for air safety, Ewing was especially puzzled by the "turning maneuver reported by the Soviet radar observers as having occurred just prior to [KE007's] arrival over Sakhalin Island."[1] How could such an accident -- that it *was* an accident Ewing insisted from the start -- have taken place? His search for an answer led him to another discovery: KE007's course over the Alaskan mainland had shortly after takeoff become a smooth Great Circle course, one that could only have been followed by an aircraft under the control of functioning Inertial Navigation Systems.

Ewing's effort to explain and reconcile these two findings led him to produce, in October, 1985, an impressively-titled monograph, "An Analysis and Scenario of Probable Cause of the Course Deviation Incidently Involving Flt. KE007 PANC-RKSS, 31 August 1983."

Stripped of some of its technical jargon, Ewing's thesis is as follows:

1. While programming KE007's INS's, flight engineer Kim Eui Dong inadvertently typed into the No. 1 INS the wrong latitude for Anchorage itself. Kim thus created an erroneous "INS position" ten degrees (289nm) east of where the aircraft was actually parked;

2. Once the aircraft was aloft over Alaska, its captain (Chun Byung-In) typed into the first waypoint "slot" in the No. 1 INS the coordinates of a waypoint other than the first waypoint on R-20 (the Bethel VOR). The idea was to place KE007 on a course that would win its crew a bonus by saving fuel. But Chun too made a typing error. This, combined with the first misprogramming, sent KE007 north of Bethel to a "hybrid waypoint" (N60°00.0′/W171°49.3′) out over the Bering Sea, and thence on its deviant course across Kamchatka and the Sea of Okhotsk to the point of the turn;

3. Shortly after committing this second programming error, Captain Chun left KE007's flight deck and remained absent for some five hours. Because his subordinates, being Orientals, did not dare to question or disturb their superior, they filed position reports as if the aircraft were on course and ignored the many warnings and anomalies that the aircraft was in fact deviating to the north;

4. As KE007 approached Sakhalin, copilot Sohn tried to insert into his (No. 2) INS the coordinates of the remaining waypoints along R-20 (NOHO, NANAC, IFH [Inkfish], MXT [Matsushima], GTC [Nigata], SEL [Seoul]. Sohn finished his insertions by typing the coordinates for SEL into the seventh waypoint "slot." But the misprogrammed command (No. 1) INS already had the aircraft flying between waypoints seven and eight (NIPPI and NOKKA). To fly to NOKKA from a new seventh waypoint that was *ahead* of the aircraft meant that KE007 would have to turn in midair and circle the globe to reach Seoul first. Only then could

it fly from Seoul to NOKKA. It was the attempt to do this that caused the aircraft to turn to the north.

Ewing, it must be borne in mind, was the only "innocent-error" theorist with a background in aviation and air navigation. His explanations of how KE007's flight crew could trebly misprogram its INS's, ignore or actually override INS warning lights, disregard other cockpit instruments, falsify its position reports and go complacently to its doom, strange though they seem, were plausible enough to persuade Seymour Hersh to make extensive use of his theories in "*The Target Is Destroyed!*" Hersh's endorsement in turn added much to Ewing's credibility.[2] This was unfortunate, because Ewing's thesis, long since disproven by both navigational analysis and the testimony of KE015's captain, Park Yong-man, was from the start a tissue of dubious operational conjectures and striking navigational errors. In what follows, we deal with both, but it is Ewing's navigational imaginings that ultimately proved his analysis valueless.

Ewing's operational scenario.
    Central to Ewing's thesis is the notion that the initialization of KE007's INS's at Anchorage was the responsibility of the most junior member of its flight crew, Flight Engineer Kim Eui Dong; and that it was Kim who, alone on the flight deck, inserted W139°00.0' instead of W149°00.0' for the aircraft's ramp position.
    The notion that Kim was alone during initialization is of the utmost importance to Ewing's theory, because it allows Ewing to "explain" how, despite clear warnings, Kim perpetuated his 10-degree programming error. Thus, Ewing would have it that after misprogramming the No. 1 INS, Kim fed the Anchorage coordinates correctly into the No. 2 and No. 3 INS's, each time pressing a button to "cancel" the amber warning lights that

immediately flashed to signal the discrepancy. Why Kim would override warning lights that might ultimately save his life, Ewing does not explain. But Kim had to have been alone, for otherwise another member of the flight crew would surely have spotted the double warning and taken remedial action.

Some airlines (e.g., TWA) do make flight engineers responsible for INS initialization -- subject to double-checking by captain and copilot.

Korean Air Lines specifically does not. In fact, KAL's B747 Operations Manual specifies that during INS initialization *both captain and copilot must be present*. The flight engineer is never permitted to undertake initialization. The copilot, in the presence of the two other crew members, initializes the INS's and inserts waypoint coordinates. The captain then calls out all waypoint locations and the copilot and the flight engineer confirm the readings.[3] Ewing gives no evidence to support his assertion that KE007's flight crew violated initialization procedure on August 31, 1983. (Kim's being the first crew member in the cockpit[4] was probably because as flight engineer he had the duty to conduct pre-flight instrument checks and supervise fuel loading.)

Secondly, Ewing's scenario depends on the crew's not having engaged the triple mix function of KE007's INS's after takeoff. Had it done so, No. 1 INS with its huge positional error would have been cut out of the navigational circuit. Nos. 2 and 3 alone would have governed KE007's actual course, which would have been the course prescribed by its flight plan.

Ewing, we recall, asserts that shortly after 1302.40Z, when KE007 received ATC clearance to "proceed direct Bethel when able," Captain Chun typed into the No. 1 INS the coordinates of a new second waypoint, one defining a leg of the course which would win the crew a bonus by saving fuel. (That in Ewing's scenario Chun entered the coordinates wrongly is, for the moment, not at issue.) Because the aircraft, after flying this leg under the control of the No. 1 INS, would have returned to R-20, there would have been no reason for Chun to enter his non-official waypoint in all three INS's.

The KAL B747 Operations Manual specifies that triple mix be engaged at or above 10,000 feet.[5]

Thirdly, Ewing postulates that soon after entering his new waypoint, Chun left KE007's flight deck to mingle with important passengers and deadheading KAL crew members, remaining absent until at least 1803Z -- a period of about five hours. Fourthly, during Chun's absence, Ewing insists that the other members of the flight crew, presumably out of blind trust in their captain, violated many other operational procedures. One example was the requirement to conduct a "gateway" or "departure" check as the aircraft passed Bethel -- in reality, 12.6nm north of Bethel -- and began the oceanic portion of its journey. Even more conspicuous was copilot Sohn's failure (according to Ewing, Sohn was "confused") to have performed a "Gross Error" check. This, utilizing the DME (Distance Measuring Equipment) complex at Bethel, is a comparison of the geographic position of the aircraft as registered on its INS's against the known position of the Bethel VOR. The supposed 289-nautical-mile misprogramming in KE007's No. 1 INS is precisely the sort of error a Gross Error Check is designed to catch.

A fifth Ewing allegation of flight-deck misbehavior, resulting from a deliberate misreading of standard KAL procedure, will be discussed later.

Finally, Chun's five-hour absence from the flight deck is an operational violation so egregious as to make even the most credulous believer in KE007's innocence doubt that it could have happened. Yet Ewing must postulate it, as he must postulate a Kim alone to cancel the INS comparator lights, because, to paraphrase Ewing, had the captain been present he would have known that something was wrong.[6]

Ewing on navigation.

In Volume I (p. 19) and elsewhere,[7] we have freely credited Ewing with being the first to note from the King Salmon and Kenai radar returns that KE007 followed a GCc across Alaska. Here, however, we must point out that in his eagerness to make this key fact fit his thesis Ewing both misreads his own finding and, more important, overlooks or disregards other significant radar evidence.

Thus, Ewing starts with the notion that a pilot "eyeballing" a Jeppesen *North Pacific High/Low and High Altitude En Route Chart* in search of a fuel-saving short-cut would by process of elimination settle on a set of coordinates marking a reporting-point for eastbound flights entering the Alaskan ADIZ (Air Defense Identification Zone): N60°00.0′/W168°00.0′.[8]

A straight edge laid across the chart from the Anchorage VOR to the above location, Ewing says, looks as if the course between the two would shave a few miles (and a substantial amount of fuel) off the standard J-501/R-20 route.[9] Accordingly, KE007's Captain Chun, after receiving clearance to fly to Bethel, started to type into the No. 1 INS the coordinates given above. He typed the latitude coordinate, N60°00.0′, into the slot for the Bethel waypoint (in Ewing's scenario, Waypoint Two). But then, "some factor could have interrupted the Captain" or else "the INS unit failed to accept the longitude component."[10] Ewing does not explain what could have distracted the captain, or why an INS otherwise functioning perfectly should have failed to accept this one coordinate. But as a result, Ewing says, Chun forgot to type in the 168-degree longitude coordinate of his fuel-saving waypoint. So the longitude entry for Bethel remained in the INS's memory along with the latitude entry for the new waypoint. The correct longitude for Bethel is W161°49.3′. *But Kim, back in Anchorage, had made a ten-degree error in initializing KE007's No. 1 INS.* So the longitude for Bethel actually resident in the No. 1 INS's memory was W171°49.3′. And so we have Ewing's "hybrid" waypoint: N60°00.0′/W171°49.3′.

Soon after this (Ewing never states exactly when), Chun supposedly typed into the NO. 1 INS the command "Zero to Two." This instantly put KE007 on the GCc defined by King Salmon and Kenai military radar, the GCc which was supposed to take the 747 to the fuel-saving waypoint but which according to Ewing took it to the "hybrid" waypoint instead and thence across Kamchatka, the Sea of Okhotsk and Sakhalin Island.

The chief problem with this version of events is that KE007 never did fly to Ewing's hybrid waypoint in the first place. We will expand on this point shortly. First, however, we must note a highly intriguing feature of the Great Circle course on which Ewing -- in due conformity with King Salmon and Kenai radars -- has KE007 flying.

If every GCc can be defined by any two points upon it, in the case at hand these would be "Zero," the exact position of KE007 at the exact instant Chun commanded it to fly to his fuel-saving waypoint, and "Two," the position of the hybrid waypoint to which it supposedly actually flew instead. But while two points suffice to define a GCc, there will of course also be an infinite number of other points upon it. As our examination of the radar returns revealed, one of the other points on this particular GCc is N61°09.1′/W150°12.3′. This is the location of the Anchorage VOR (Very High Frequency Omni Range) navigational radio beacon, a powerful navigational aid for aviators in the Anchorage region.

Ewing does not explain in his analysis how Captain Chun managed to turn onto a westward GCc defined not only by

"Zero" and "Two" but equally by the Anchorage VOR and "Two." In a letter in answer to our query on the issue, he offered a rather odd account of his reasoning:

> What I did was to recover the probable point of initiation of a GCc by taking an approach plate [map of the Anchorage airport] and my thumb and a lot of Kentucky windage and guessing . . . and, what the hell, the [Anchorage] VOR was there, about a half a thumbwidth away, and . . . I just decided to use those [coordinates].[11]

Later in the same letter, he further muddied this explanation:

> In point of fact I don't think that the VOR, per se, or its' [sic] coordinates, per se, were ever an element of the case beyond being located, coincidentally, within a mile or two of the point where [Chun] was cleared direct BET [Bethel].[12]

But no matter what Ewing claimed he did or did not do with his thumb, the coordinates of the Anchorage VOR clearly and unmistakably are "an element of the case." In a nutshell, Ewing was using an unimportant fact, that the Anchorage VOR was "within a mile or two" of where KE007 received its clearance to Bethel, to mask an important fact, that *as the radar returns independently confirm*, coordinates of the VOR define a point on the Great Circle course onto which KE007 turned to fly across Alaska.

Rather than asserting that this fact was merely an amazing coincidence, it would have made better sense for Ewing to assume that it was evidence of deliberate navigational design.

That is, that KE007's Captain Chun (or someone else) made use of the Anchorage VOR as a "root" or starting-point of a preplanned GCc. In this case, the coordinates of the VOR would have been Waypoint One, those of Ewing's putative fuel-saving Waypoint Two. Then, as soon as the command "One to Two" had been typed into the No. 1 INS, the aircraft would have turned gently onto the course.[13]

Ewing, however, was not free to make this common-sense assumption, *because according to his own scenario KE007's No. 1 INS contained Kim's ten-degree error.*

This meant that the command to fly the 747 from "One to Two" would have been entered in an INS which had previously accepted that the longitude of Waypoint One was some 252 nautical miles *ahead* of the aircraft. And so, to fulfill the command, KE007 would first have to have turned in midair to place Waypoint One behind it and then flown *eastward* across Canada, across the Atlantic, across northern Europe and in effect around the globe to reach Waypoint Two. This, as Ewing knew well from the King Salmon and Kenai radar returns, never occurred. So he had no choice but to make do with "Kentucky windage" and the unsupported and unlikely assertion that the Anchorage VOR cropped up on KE007's course by sheer happenstance.

Other peculiarities mark Ewing's version of KE007's overland GCc. Thus, central to his scenario is the finding that this GCc actually flew the aircraft to the hybrid waypoint, N60°00.0'/W171°49.3'. But a LOTOL (longitude-to-latitude) test[14] of the GCc depicted by the King Salmon and Kenai radar data reveals that the course crosses W171°49.3' at N60°01.6'. The 1.6nm difference is small, but in commercial air navigation terms it is significant.

Much more significant is the relationship of Ewing's hybrid waypoint to another geographic location, that of the VHF Air

Traffic Control Relay station on St. Paul Island, at N57°09.5'/W170°13.6'. Given the height of the station's antenna above sea level (657 feet), we have determined that a commercial aircraft flying at 31,000 feet (KE007's assigned flight level) would probably be within range of the relay station at any distance up to 230 miles -- and would thus be able to communicate directly with Anchorage Air Traffic Control.[15]

ICAO is slightly more conservative. "The radio coverage from the [St. Paul relay station] was approximately 175nm in all directions."[16]

Ewing's hybrid waypoint is 177.6 nautical miles north northwest of St. Paul Island. Yet KE007 had to relay its NABIE position report to Anchorage via its "sister flight," KE015.

Ewing explains this by asserting that "the flight's inability to secure VHF communication through various Anchorage Center remote sites barely deserves comment" because "VHF communication in this area [is] so spotty."[17] Ewing offers no explanation of what he means by "spotty": the term could cover everything from faulty cable connections through iced-over antennas to broken-down slave transceivers. Nor does he put forward evidence that VHF communication in the region of R-20 was impaired on the morning of August 31, 1983. We might note here that atmospherics have no effect on VHF communication. We should also note that R-20 is an FAA-certified transoceanic airway, one which by definition must afford aircraft highly dependable ground communications facilities. Further, on the morning of August 31, 1983, no other aircraft within radio range of St. Paul Island -- including KE015 -- had trouble contacting Anchorage ATC direct. In a word, we agree with ICAO that "it can be reasonably assumed that KE007 was outside the coverage of the St. Paul [relay station]."[18] The simplest explanation of why KE007 had to relay its message is that it never overflew the hybrid waypoint at all.[19] According to Ewing, however, once KE007 reached the hybrid waypoint it turned slightly northward and rejoined the GCc it would have followed had Kim's ten-degree error been the only misprogramming inflicted on its long-suffering No. 1 INS. It then flew this course across the Bering Sea to Kamchatka and beyond.

Ewing mentioned Kamchatka only once in his analysis, in a passing reference to the untrustworthiness of weather radar in its ground-mapping mode.[20] His circumspection is understandable. It saved him from having to deal with an unpleasant but inescapable fact. Namely, that the ten-degree-error course on which he insists KE007 flew would cross Kamchatka some 30 nautical miles to the north of the course the U.S. State Department and the Soviet Air Defense Force agree the aircraft actually did follow across the peninsula.

Ewing on operations revisited: the turn over the Sea of Okhotsk.

On Route R-20, the northernmost of the five Northern Pacific (NOPAC) transoceanic routes, the seven compulsory reporting points at the time of the KE007 disaster were Bethel, NABIE, NEEVA, NIPPI, NOKKA, NOHO and NANAC. These points are also waypoints at which course changes ("leg-switches") take place. The four non-compulsory reporting points were CAIRN, NUKKS, NINNO and NYTIM.[21] In westbound order, the sequence of all eleven points is CAIRN, BETHEL, NABIE, NUKKS, NEEVA, NINNO, NIPPI, NYTIM, NOKKA, NOHO, NANAC.

After passing these points on R-20, an aircraft bound for Seoul would fly via three others, IFH (Inkfish), MXT (Matsushima) and GTC (Niigata) to SEL (Seoul) itself.

The memory-banks of the INS's aboard KE007 allow the

input of up to nine waypoint positions at the start of a flight. If a given route has more than nine waypoints, the additional waypoints have to be typed in during the course of the flight, into the "slots" of waypoints the aircraft has already passed. Ewing contended that at about 1807Z, as KE007 approached Sakhalin Island, copilot Sohn's No. 2 INS was displaying "FROM-8 TO-9," meaning that as far as Sohn knew the aircraft was proceeding from NYTIM to NOKKA -- that is, "if the crew had numbered the waypoints on their flight plan in a conventional manner."[22] This, Ewing said, would have been the time for Sohn to load the remaining waypoints, "so that the flight would not experience an interruption in navigation as it passed Waypoint #9."

Accordingly, Sohn allegedly began to type in new waypoint coordinates. "With normal numbering," Ewing says,

> Noho would have become the 'new' Waypoint #1, the Anyang VOR (SEL) would have been Waypoint #7 and the Seoul Airport (also SEL) on the flight plan would have been Waypoint #8.[23]

But unknown to Sohn, the command (No. 1) INS contained Kim's ten-degree error. So it would sense that it had flown KE007 past Ewing's Waypoint 7 [NIPPI] and was en route to his Waypoint 8 [NYTIM]. The instant Sohn entered a new Waypoint 7 that was ahead of the aircraft (SEL), "the faulted #1 INS would have sensed that it was now instructed to navigate FROM-SEL TO-NYTIM."[24] To do this, *KE007 would have to perform exactly the same maneuver that Ewing struggles so hard to resist having it perform between Anchorage and his hybrid waypoint.* That is, turn in midflight to place Seoul behind it, circumnavigate the globe to reach Seoul first and then proceed from Seoul to NYTIM.

And in Ewing's view of events, when KE007 did start its northward turn, only prompt action by Sohn prevented it from executing a complete reversal of course and flying back toward Kamchatka.

But the facts about KAL flight-deck operations cast serious doubt on this critical piece of Ewing's scenario.

We must bear in mind that the Ewing interpretation of KE007's turn hinges on the notion that its flight crew had entered NIPPI as Waypoint Seven, NYTIM as Waypoint Eight and NOKKA as Waypoint Nine, requiring the insertion of new waypoints as KE007's No. 2 INS signalled the approach of the ninth and last of the original waypoints. This, according to Ewing, would have been "conventional numbering."

But would it?

For these waypoints to be assigned these numbers, KE007's crew would have had to have entered in its INS's *every single one* of the reporting-points, compulsory and non-compulsory, along R-20. And even then, the numbers fail to work out properly: there are simply too few R-20 waypoints to meet Ewing's need. A glance at the list will make our meaning clear:

Waypoint	Waypoint Number
BETHEL/Hybrid Waypoint	1
NABIE	?
NUKKS	?
NEEVA	?
NINNO	?
	?
NIPPI	7
NYTIM	8
NOKKA	9

Clearly, where Ewing requires nine waypoints, R-20 can supply only eight.

In his analysis, Ewing never gives a complete list of the waypoints prior to NIPPI, or otherwise accounts for this anomaly. But Seymour Hersh, in "*The Target Is Destroyed*" asserted that "many international pilots routinely use Cairn Mountain [CRN] . . . as the first waypoint, *as does Ewing's scenario.*"[25] [Emphasis added.] Cairn Mountain, 162 nautical miles southwest of Anchorage, is the site of a Non-directional Low Frequency Radio Beacon (NDB), which can indeed be used as a navigational aid. But it is neither a compulsory nor a non-compulsory reporting-point. Nor, whatever Hersh and Ewing say, is it "routinely used" as a waypoint by major air carriers flying J-501/R-20.

It is hard to resist the thought that Ewing, urgently needing one more waypoint to make up the total of nine which would flesh out his theory, plucked Cairn Mountain from the route map and pressed it into service, as Hersh affirms, as KE007's Waypoint One.[26]

More compelling still is the comment of Vernon C. Stone. Stone, a retired British Airways supervisor-pilot, was a member of the British Airways team that trained the initial cadre of KAL 747 pilots. Asked about waypoint insertions, Stone said that KAL pilots were taught: "The fewer the waypoints the better." (That is, the fewer the opportunities for error.) Sugwon Kang, a Korean-born political scientist with a profound interest in the KE007 disaster, told us independently that his correspondence with Korean Airlines pilots confirms Stone's statement. Standard KAL practice is to insert *only* compulsory reporting-points:[27] the use of non-compulsory points is rare. It is certainly not a "conventional" practice.

If KE007's flight crew had indeed followed conventional KAL practice, it would have entered into its INS's at Anchorage: 1) BET (Bethel), 2) NABIE, 3) NEEVA, 4) NIPPI, 5) NOKKA, 6) NOHO, 7) NANAC, 8) IFH (Inkfish) and 9)

MXT (Matsushima). Only two more waypoint entries would have been required, and these would have been made far downline and at least an hour later than the 1807Z at which Ewing alleges they were made.

And so, we must seek some different explanation for KE007's northward turn east of Sakhalin.

Conclusion.

In his account of KE007's turn as in his presentation of its supposed multiple INS misprogrammings, Ewing misreads, misstates and sometimes suppresses details of KAL operating procedures which are clearly spelled out in his avowed major source, "Attachment B" to *State Letter LE 4/19.4-83/130, Report of ICAO Fact-Finding Investigation, December 1983.*

In his elaborate navigational scenario, Ewing selected those elements of the extensive navigational and communications evidence that fit his thesis of an aircraft innocently astray and ignored those elements that call this thesis into question. Two telling examples out of many we can name are his disregard of the issue of leg-by-leg air speeds and his calculated neglect of the entire middle portion of the flight, that during which KE007 transited the Buffer Zone and approached and crossed the Kamchatka Peninsula.

In November, 1986, Park Yong-man, captain of KE015, put Ewing's scenario to rest in an interview in the South Korean monthly *Wolgan Chosun.* He first demolished Ewing's notion that KE007's Captain Chun had been absent from the flight deck for five hours, asserting that he himself had spoken with Chun more than once during the period in question. Years later, Park's assertion would be lent credibility by the transcripts of communications between KE007 and KE015 taken from the Cockpit Voice Recorder of the downed aircraft.

Park rejected the idea that KE007 was on a "spy flight."

But he also dismissed as "laughable conjecture" Ewing's theory that Chun inserted an (erroneous) shortcut into KE007's INS's in order to win a bonus by saving fuel.

NOTES

1. Harold H. Ewing, "An Analysis and Scenario of Probable Cause of the Course Deviation Incident Involving Flt. KE007 PANC-RKSS, 31 August 1983," [hereafter "Analysis and Scenario"], p. E-2.

2. Pearson, for example, felt he must concede that "Ewing came up with a theory that is consistent with the facts." Pearson, *KAL007: The Cover-Up*, p. 343.

3. ICAO Air Navigation Commission, *Final Report of Investigation*, p. 21.

4. As reported by Hersh, not Ewing. See Hersh, *"Target Is Destroyed"*, p. 199.

5. Triple mix was engaged. See Vol. I, pp. 19-20.

6. Ewing, "Analysis and Scenario," p. E-19. Also, Hersh, *op. cit.*, p. 223.

7. See esp. Allardyce and Gollin, "Various Perceptions of the Death of KAL007," in *Et Cetera*, Summer 1987, p. 133.

8. Ewing, "Analysis and Scenario," p. 16.

9. In fact, it would save 6.9 nautical miles (Ewing mistakenly states on page E-16 that it would save "a little over a mile") and forty-five seconds of flight time at Ewing's assumed M.840, resulting in a saving of 354 pounds of fuel. Note that KE007's fuel load at takeoff was 263,700 pounds.

10. Ewing, "Analysis and Scenario," p. 17.

11. Harold H. Ewing, letter to R. W. Allardyce, October 31, 1985, p. 1.

12. *Loc. cit.*

13. KE007 did indeed join a preplanned GCC of which the Anchorage VOR was Waypoint One. Waypoint Two, however, was not Ewing's hybrid. See Vol. I p. 21, p. 38.

14. A LOTOL test, done on the navigational computer, supplies the precise latitude at which a given Great Circle course crosses any degree of longitude.

15. We are grateful to Michel Brun for correcting our earlier calculation of 205nm. John Keppel to Richard Witkin, letter dated March 16, 1992, and enclosure.

16. *ICAO Report*, p. 19.

17. Ewing, "Analysis and Scenario," p. 20.

18. *ICAO Report*, p.38.

19. For our determination of KE007's actual course and distance from St. Paul Island, see Vol. I, pp. 38-39.

20. Ewing, "Analysis and Scenario," p. 21.

21. R-20 is a westbound airway. The points are listed in westbound order. Compulsory reporting points are locations at which flight crews are required to make position reports to the Air Traffic Control center in the appropriate Flight Information Region. Non-compulsory points are intermediate locations at which position checks may be made and reports filed but at which these are not mandatory.

22. Ewing, "Analysis and Scenario," p. 22.

23. *Ibid.*, p. 23.

24. *Loc. cit.*

25. Hersh, *"Target Is Destroyed"*, p. 202.

26. *Loc. cit.*

27. However, Caj E. Frostell, the senior ICAO official who worked on the 1983 *ICAO Report* and led the team that produced the *1993 ICAO Report*, disagrees with Stone and Kang (and ourselves). "... the crew on the KAL flight from Anchorage to Seoul on which I travelled on 3 Oct 1983, entered all the reporting points.... Why would the KAL practice have changed so soon after the accident?" Caj Frostell-Richard Witkin, enclosure in letter c. November 21, 1991. The presence of Mr. Frostell on the flight deck might well -- we think -- have prompted the change.

BUFFER ZONE ADDENDUM

The Alaskan Buffer Zone is an irregular, boomerang-shaped strip of airspace lying off the Alaskan coast just inside the western boundary of a much larger area, the Alaskan DEWIZ, or "Distant Early Warning Identification Zone." A small wedge of the Buffer Zone south and west of Nome is also contained in the innermost envelope of Alaskan airspace, the Alaskan ADIZ, or "Air Defense Identification Zone." (See map.)

The Buffer Zone is described and discussed in the *United States Government Flight Information Publication, Alaska Supplement*.[1] Its geographic coordinates are given as:

N58°00.0'	W180°00.0'
N60°00.0'	W180°00.0'
N65°00.0'	W169°00.0'
N72°00.0'	W169°00.0'
N72°00.0'	W167°00.0'
N62°30.0'	W167°00.0'

The Alaskan Buffer Zone was on the morning of August 31, 1983, and is even today, an exceedingly dangerous place. Immediately to its west, aviation charts still depict a "Non-Free Flying Zone." Most charts carry a printed advisory that aircraft entering the Non-Free Flying Zone are liable to be fired upon (by Russian interceptors) without warning.

Many investigators of the Soviet downing of KE007 have raised the general question of why the U.S., with its long-range military radars, electronic listening-posts, intelligence aircraft and other powerful monitoring installations, failed to warn KE007 that it was off-course and heading into harm's way. But very few have noticed that the aircraft's actual course took it into and through the Buffer Zone. As we point out,[2] its time in transit was at least 17 minutes, the distance covered within the Zone, a minimum of 130.4 nautical miles. As we also point out, the question of how and why this penetration could have happened has elicited some weirdly contradictory answers. But the usual tactic of U.S. officials and their allies when asked about the Buffer Zone has been to circle the wagons and pretend away its existence.

To cite the classic non-answer, James Edward Oberg, in one of his many spirited defenses of the "innocently lost" argument, concedes with annoyance that "'Why didn't we warn it?' . . . is the key question used and abused by Soviet commentators, right from the start." Oberg then runs down what he calls "the available U.S. sensors" and decides that none of them, not the FAA nor the Air Force (he claims it had no "agreement" with the FAA and hence no mandate to monitor civilian air traffic, a claim we will test shortly) nor the COBRA DANE radar on Shemya Island nor the PAVE PAWS radar at Wakkanai nor the "RC-135" (he acknowledges that there was one) off Kamchatka could have spotted the errant airliner, much less warned it. But in his "careful catalog of actual U.S. assets," Oberg makes no mention at all of the Buffer Zone.[3]

The realities of air traffic control in and near Alaska in August, 1983 (and today), make a sorry joke out of this omission.

Given the type and density of air traffic in the 49th state, where roads are few and distances huge, where the airplane is the transportation method of necessity for everyone from oil-company personnel and professional fish-finders to ministers and pastors serving their scattered flocks, the need for strict air traffic regulation becomes obvious. It becomes even more obvious when one realizes also that the Alaska Air Defense

Command is one of the biggest and busiest of this country's air-defense outposts, adding scores of military flights daily to the hundreds of civilian flights in the region. Indeed, regulation and enforcement in general are so stringent that the regulations governing the Buffer Zone, which as we shall see are Draconian, are almost beside the point. We can start with the fact that in 1983 as now, every aircraft proceeding westbound from the Alaskan mainland was by definition either operating within or flying through the envelope of airspace called the Alaskan Air Defense Identification Zone. The *Alaska Supplement* describes the ADIZ as ". . . an airspace of defined dimensions within which certain rules for the security control of aircraft are mandatory in the interest of National Security [*sic*]."[4]

One of the most basic of these rules is the one that requires all international airline flights operating under ICAO regulations -- as KE007 certainly was operating on the night it was destroyed -- to file IFR (Instrument Flight Rules) flight plans and to obtain IFR clearances from their Air Traffic Control Centers.

The allowable tolerances for adherence to FAA/ICAO IFR flight plans are strict:

1. Time. Plus or minus five minutes from an estimate over a reporting point. (Three minutes for scheduled passenger aircraft over oceanic reporting points.)

2. Distance. Ten nautical miles from centerline of proposed route within the ADIZ. [Over the Alaskan mainland.] Twenty nautical miles within the DEWIZ.

3. Altitude deviation. None unless an amended
    air traffic clearance is obtained or, if operating
    where no air traffic clearance is required, prior
    notice is given to appropriate aeronautical
    facility.[5]

Where there are rules, there is enforcement. Enforcement
of the Alaskan air traffic rules is largely managed through a
process known as Flight Plan Correlation.[6]

Under this procedure, FAA Air Traffic Control feeds the
flight plans of *all* civilian aircraft flying in the Alaska
ADIZ/DEWIZ into the computers of the Air Force's NORAD
Regional Operations Control Center. (NORAD stands for
"North American Air Defense Command.") The technicians at
ROCC compare the actual radar tracks of their flights with
their flight plans. It makes no difference whether an aircraft is
inbound or outbound: if the radar return fails to match the
flight plan -- an uncommon occurrence, given that most pilots
know well what might ensue -- ROCC contacts the appropriate
FAA Air Traffic Control facility. "To see," as the head of
ROCC put it at the time, "if the aircraft is on a flight plan but
out of acceptable limits. If they identify the track it will be
declared 'friendly'; if not, it will either remain 'pending' or be
made 'unknown.'"[7] In the latter two cases, it will be subject to
whatever action--including air interception--ROCC deems
appropriate. (NORAD headquarters at Cheyenne Mountain,
Colorado, is also notified of all mismatches.)

From the above, it is indisputable that the Air Force's
Alaska Air Command can, does and in 1983 did monitor the
entirety of the Alaskan Domestic ADIZ and Alaskan DEWIZ.
In 1983, such monitoring would have been done largely through
the twelve units of the ground-based SEEK IGLOO Distant
Early Warning system, possibly supplemented at the extremity

of their ranges by airborne radar.

With this system of rules, enforcement procedures and monitoring capability in mind, we can now profitably focus on the Buffer Zone.

The *Alaska Supplement* minces no words about who is allowed into the Buffer Zone and on what types of flights:

> The following is a summary of the procedures which apply to aircraft assigned to or under the operational control of ANR/AAC [Alaskan NORAD Regional Control Center/Alaska Air Command], which are operating in the Alaskan Buffer Zone.
>
> A. Penetration flights into the Alaskan Buffer Zone by USAF aircraft require specific authorization. At no time does this approval constitute authority to enter the Nonfree Flying Zone.
>
> B. Pilots filing flight plans to a destination within the Buffer Zone will include an alternate airport which is outside the Buffer Zone. Pilots will include the statement "PADRA, BUFFER ZONE TRAFFIC, TOP COVER 64" in the remarks section of the flight plan. [PADRA means "Pass To Air Defense Radar."]
>
> C. During the duration of the mission within the Buffer Zone, TOP COVER 64 aircraft will use USAF Radar Assistance Service as outlined in this publication.[8]

D. USAF aircraft which anticipate operation within the Buffer Zone must have a fully operational two-way radio and IFF [special "Identification Friend or Foe" transponder that is interrogated by radio and fully read by radar].

USAF Radar Assistance Service, as a separate section explains,

is designed to assist aircraft in flight to avoid areas of potentially hazardous conditions such as weather, anti-aircraft artillery zones, restricted areas, warning areas, etc.[9]

This last is the Air Force's courteous way of saying that if you want to operate in the Buffer Zone you will please *ask* to be identified and tracked -- willy-nilly, you *will* be identified and tracked -- by USAF ACW (Aircraft Control and Warning) radar. The explanation is followed by a list of the radio frequencies, civilian and military, on which you can make your request. Nothing is said in the *Alaska Supplement* because nothing needs to be said, about what would happen if you should show up on ACW radar in the Buffer Zone *without* having let the Air Force know who or what you were.

The Buffer Zone Procedures, to give them their official name, are aimed almost exclusively at USAF aircraft. Their opening sentence refers specifically to "aircraft assigned to or under the operational control of ANR/AAC." This category could be and probably is expandable to include certain types of civilian aircraft (for instance, those ferrying civilian maintenance personnel to and from their work on USAF installations in the Zone). The Procedures also indicate, somewhat obscurely, that

"Other aircraft are encouraged to coordinate with Alaskan Norad Control prior to conducting operations in the Buffer Zone."[10] What other aircraft? Our assumption is that the reference is to other U.S. military aircraft (e.g., Navy P-3 Orion anti-submarine aircraft, Army helicopters, USAF aircraft from other commands). As for civilian aircraft *not* under military control, the Buffer Zone is virtually forbidden territory.

When KE007 passed abeam Bethel at 1350.09Z on the morning of August 31, 1983, it was already 12.6 nautical miles north of course. By about 1403Z, it had reached the point over the ocean (N60°37.9'/W165°45.0')[11] where it turned slightly northward to make good its course toward Kamchatka.

And at this point, about fifteen minutes and 119.7nm beyond Bethel, it was about 26nm north of the R-20 airway which was its flight-plan route.

The tapes of the two USAF DEW/ACW radars that would have spotted both this distance deviation -- clearly in excess of "allowable tolerances" -- and the turn that would cause the deviation to grow and grow were "routinely" recycled by the USAF within a few days of the disaster, and their content destroyed. (The radars in question were those at Cape Newenham and Cape Romanzof.) The fact of the destruction is suggestive, to say the least. Whether or not a third DEW radar (at Dillingham, 145.7nm SE of Bethel) also tracked KE007 as it exited the ADIZ, entered the DEWIZ and continued its deviation is not known. Nor is it known what other radars were employed at the time on Flight Plan Correlation. But that the Air Force somehow failed to notice what its entire system is designed to flag and correct is preposterous.

The Obergs and Klasses and Ewings and others echoing the State Department's "innocently lost" refrain would further have us believe that KE007 flew unobserved through the Alaskan

DEWIZ for another thirty-five minutes and 270 nautical miles, passing *some 60nm north* of its proper R-20 waypoint at NABIE.

And next, whatever these same commentators think or say, KE007 flew on into the Buffer Zone. This pocket of airspace, to elaborate on what has already been set forth at length, is the U.S. equivalent of the Soviet Nonfree Flying Zone. Even USAF interceptors require special permission to be there. Nothing can land there without clearance. Everything that flies there is tracked and is required to maintain continuous radio contact with the USAF warning radar network. Anything that cannot do so because of radio or transponder failure must leave the Zone on an eastward heading or else be intercepted and either forced to land or shot down. Nevertheless, we are expected to swallow that a Korean 747 wandered innocently into and through this forbidden, forbidding environment for at least 17.2 minutes, again while no one noticed. Of all of the many pieces of disinformation put forth by or on behalf of the U.S. in connection with the KE007 affair, this must be at once the silliest and the most cynical.

The real answer to the question, "Why didn't the U.S. contact KE007 to warn it?" is "There was no need." KE007's flight crew knew where it was and where it was going, and the guardians of Alaskan airspace knew to let it pass.

NOTES

1. To be referred to hereafter as *Alaska Supplement*: p. 171. Page references are to the edition in effect as of 15 March 1984. ADIZ, DEWIZ and Buffer Zone Procedures in this edition are those in effect on 31 August 1983.

2. Vol. I, p. 68.

3. James Edward Oberg, "Sense, Nonsense, and Pretense on the KAL-007 Tragedy," November 8, 1984, pp. 24-28. Similarly, Harold H. Ewing, in his analysis of KE007's flight, totally ignores the Buffer Zone.

4. *Alaska Supplement*, p. 172.

5. *Ibid.*, p. 178.

6. Our outline of Flight Plan Correlation is based on the account of Lieutenant General Bruce K. Brown, Commander, NORAD Alaska Regional Operations Center in "Presentation to the Committee on Foreign Affairs, Subcommittee on East Asia and Pacific Affairs, United States Senate," October 6, 1983," p. 4; and on "Radar Against Soviet Air Attack to Run Part Time," in *The New York Times*, May 28, 1991, p. A14.

7. Lieut. Gen. Bruce K. Brown, "Briefing," p. 4.

8. *Alaska Supplement*, p. 172.

9. *Ibid.*, p. 165.

10. *Ibid.*, p. 171.

11. This fix is derived from the course layout based on the data about KE007's downline positions released to us by the Central Intelligence Agency. See Vol. I, p. 64. The position is some 26.6nm to the west of the fix (N60°46.6'/W165°00.0') drawn from our original course layout. See Vol. I, p. 40.

ETP ADDENDUM

During his pre-flight planning, KE007's Captain Chun Byung-in[1] made a number of notations on the copy of the computer-generated flight plan he left with the KAL dispatcher at Anchorage International Airport. One of the most significant of these is found about one-third of the way down the page on the right-hand side. The note says simply:

ETP 1501 nm
3 HR 22 min

It has widely been assumed that Chun's "ETP" stands for "Equal Time Point." This would make it mean the geographic location on an air journey where, with the forecast winds taken into account, the same amount of time will be needed to proceed to the next usable airport as would be needed to return to the point of departure. (Most people like to call this location, remembering old aviation movies, "the point of no return" and to associate it with the point beyond which the pilot's fuel supply will no longer be enough to get him -- or her -- back to base safely.)

The trouble with this explanation is that it is wrong. But as is often true of aspects of the KE007 disaster, the right explanation is much more evident (and meaningful) once we dispose of the wrong one.

Thus, the formula used to calculate the Equal Time Point is known to pilots as the "radius of action" formula. The formula can be set up to yield a result either in terms of distance or of time:

$$\frac{(D \text{ } or \text{ } M)Gb}{Go+Gb} = \text{Distance } or \text{ Time to ETP}$$

where D=Total distance of flight; M=Total time of flight; Gb=Ground speed back to origin; Go=Ground speed to destination.

Today's jet airliners have such great range that their pilots almost never to have to worry about having enough fuel to fly them back to their starting-points. But there are other occasions, ranging from electrical or electronic malfunctions to engine failures to passenger illnesses to onboard fire, that would cause a prudent pilot to need to know whether to land short of his final destination or even return to the point of origin. So working the formula to produce an Equal Time Point is a handy exercise; and doing the computations on the ground before takeoff may mean not having to do them under emergency conditions in midflight.

With this in mind, we can trace the steps KE007's Captain Chun would have had to follow to calculate the Equal Time Point for his flight from Anchorage International Airport to Kimpo Airport, Seoul.

Captain Chun's copy of the flight plan set the total time for the flight at seven hours and fifty-three minutes. The total distance to be flown was 3,566 nautical miles. The average wind component for the westbound flight was minus 26 knots. (Note that this is a *head wind* for the westbound flight, but a *tail wind* for purposes of computing ground speed back, or eastbound, to Anchorage).

The flight was planned at the mandatory speed of M.840. This translates into a True Air Speed (TAS) of 490 knots.

Applying the radius of action formula, Chun would first multiply total distance (3,566nm) by ground speed back, which, adding the 26-knot tail wind to the 490-knot True Air Speed, is

516. The product is 1,840,056. This must be divided, according to the formula, by the sum of the ground speeds out (490 minus 26, or 464) and back (516), which is 980. The result is 1,877.6, the distance in nautical miles from Anchorage to the Equal Time Point. By dividing this distance by the ground speed out (464), Chun would arrive at the flying time needed to reach the Equal Time Point, which is four hours and three minutes.

Unhappily, these figures do not jibe with, or even come close to, the "1501nm/3hr 22 min" Chun wrote on his flight plan. Whatever he was doing, Chun was not calculating an Equal Time Point between Anchorage and Seoul.

What was Chun doing?

The twists and turns of the road to the answer begin at a point obvious to aviation professionals but perhaps less so to others: Chun really had no need at all to compute an Equal Time Point based on the Anchorage-Seoul journey. If KE007 had run into grave trouble over the Bering Sea or the North Pacific, many alternative emergency landing fields were available. For example, the US Naval Station at Adak in the Andreanoff Group of the Aleutian Islands is 1,190nm east of Anchorage and about 3,101nm from Seoul. Its runways and ground support equipment will readily accommodate a 747. Similarly, the USAF air station on Shemya Island, 403nm west of Adak, is roughly 1,400nm from Anchorage and 2,400 from Tokyo, which places it about halfway along KE007's assigned R-20 flight path. It too can handle a jumbo jet. In case of emergency, KE007 could have even have found safety at one of several Soviet airports on the Kamchatka Peninsula. If the emergency had developed as the aircraft approached Japan, airports in the Soviet Kuriles would have been accessible, as of course would those on the east coast of Japan proper.

This last consideration led us to review Chun's notations in the light of aviation economics. As we have just seen, in case of serious trouble Chun and his colleagues could choose from many alternatives on or near their route. But if some lesser problem made it necessary for KE007 to turn back to Anchorage, the doubling-back would be shorter and less expensive if Chun's Equal Time Point were based not on Seoul but on the first available airport west of the ocean. This, by geographical logic, Chun would have sought along the east coasts of Hokkaido and Honshu. To find what he found, we need only dissect his algebra, a simple enough task. Or so we thought at the start.

We began with his answer in nautical miles and worked the radius of action formula backward to derive a "total distance" from Anchorage:

$$\frac{1501 \times 980}{516} = 2851$$

Clearly, whichever Japanese airport is 2,851nm from Anchorage was the airport of Chun's choice.

Unfortunately, there is none.

The airport at Matsushima is 2,841nm from Anchorage. But it is not listed as capable of handling a 747. The USAF station at Misawa can accommodate a 747, but its distance from Anchorage is 2,711.5nm.

That there was no obvious candidate was puzzling enough. And then we made another disquieting discovery. When we tried to relate Chun's 1501nm to the three hours and twenty-two minutes of his time notation, we found that the radius of action formula required the use of a head wind not of the 26 knots on KE007's flight plan but of 45 knots! Thus, as noted above, a M.840 True Air Speed of 490 knots reduced by 26 knots produces a ground speed of 464 knots. But had KE007 covered ground at this speed for Chun's three hours and twenty-two minutes, it would have traveled not 1,501nm but 1,562nm. Conversely, to cover only 1,501nm in three hours and twenty-two minutes calls for a ground speed of 446 knots. If KE007's True Air Speed at M.840 was 490 knots, Chun must have based his Equal Time Point computation -- if indeed he was computing an Equal Time Point in the first place -- on a wind component of 45 knots.

Accepting that Chun had good reason for doing this, we then reworked the radius of action calculations using the revised Ground speed out (Go) of 445k and Ground speed back (Gb) of 535k:

a) 1,501 x 980 = 1,470,980

b) $\dfrac{1,470,908}{535}$ = 2,749.9nm

Miyako, a town on the northeast coast of Honshu, is 2,747.7nm from Anchorage. Miyako, moreover, is listed in the flight information directory covering Japan as the site of a VOR (Very High Frequency Omni Range) radio beacon.

No doubt it was this fact, coupled with his own version of the above calculations, that led Harold H. Ewing to state with characteristic assertiveness in a letter to another investigator of the KE007 downing that

> [t]he scribbled notes on the flight plan left at Anchorage refer [in part] to . . . the ETP, or Equal Time Point, between Anchorage and Miyako, the next nearest airfield on the other side of the ocean . . . Your unfamiliarity with these flight plans and thus, the meaning of any notes made upon them, is made clear by your comment in your book . . . .[2]

For all of this display of expertise, however, Ewing overlooked one crucial fact: according to Jeppesen Sanderson, the recognized source of aviation information worldwide, there is no airport at Miyako.[3]

James Edward Oberg, in a May 3, 1988, updating of his 1984 and 1986 essays on KE007, stated with *his* usual self-assurance that

> Captain Chun's notes actually appear to refer to the 'Equal Time Point' precisely on his planned track, and the flight time to that point, halfway between Anchorage and Narita, the main Japanese airfield . . .[4]

Tokyo, it is true, is 3,003.7nm from Anchorage via an unbroken Great Circle course, and Chun's 1,501nm is almost one-half of this distance. But as we have seen, Equal Time Point calculations are based not only upon distance but upon windage, a factor Oberg seems to have overlooked; and as we have also seen, three hours and twenty-two minutes would have been KE007's "flight time to that point" only against a head wind 19 knots faster than the one on Chun's flight plan. Oberg also neglected to point out that R-20, Chun's supposed "planned route," is not 3,003.7nm long. (Nor, of course, is it an unbroken GCc.) It is, as noted above, 3,566nm long. Nor did Chun's "planned route" lead to "Narita, the main Japanese airfield." As Oberg seems temporarily to have forgotten, KE007's destination was Seoul.

Even after a diligent search, we were no more able than Ewing and Oberg to locate an airport either 2,851 or 2,765 nautical miles from Anchorage. Accordingly, we were forced to consider the possibility that Captain Chun's "1501nm" was not the result of an algebraic calculation but rather a distance Chun already had in mind, a distance *along a preplanned course other than R-20 that he knew he would be following.*

In the third chapter of Volume I we trace in detail two possible courses that KE007 could have flown from beyond Bethel to its landfall on the east coast of the Kamchatka Peninsula. One is the "Track Y" GCc of our original work. The other is the modification of this flight path made necessary by the release of intelligence data about KE007's locations at 1551Z, 1635Z and 1706Z. We remain convinced that on either course, KE007 at 1542Z turned onto a 320-degree (True) northward heading, and that at 1551Z, it made a hard left turn onto a 220-degree (True) southwesterly heading. Had it followed the "Track Y" course until 1542Z, these turns would have taken it at 1620Z to a point 78.8 nautical miles from its point of intrusion over Kamchatka.

At 1622Z -- three hours and twenty-two minutes to the second after its 1300Z departure from Anchorage -- KE007 on this track would have been at N55°18.8'/E162°37.6', a location 1,501 nautical miles from the Anchorage VOR. The location is just east of the Asian Coastal Buffer Zone surrounding Kamchatka. Three minutes later, KE007 penetrated the Coastal Buffer Zone. Five minutes after that, KE007 entered over Kamchatka.

On the more southerly track laid out to accommodate the intelligence data, KE007 at 1622Z (the Equal Time Point) would have been at N55°56.6'/E164°26.2'. The total direct distance from the Anchorage VOR would have been 1,429nm, not 1,501nm, and the aircraft would have been about flying southwest parallel to and some 15nm from the edge of the Coastal Buffer Zone.

It seems indisputable to us that the notes on the flight plan referred to the time and distance needed to reach one or the other of the above locations. This strong likelihood, however, still leaves two questions to be answered. The first and most important is one we have already encountered in the very different "Equal Time Point" context. Namely, why did Chun feel that he had to allow three hours and twenty-two minutes to cover the distance, be it 1,501nm or 1,429nm, to his 1622Z location off Kamchatka?

The answer we believe correct is that the windage along the course Chun was planning to fly was not the 26-knot head wind of the R-20 flight plan. An abundance of evidence exists to substantiate this fact. Using ICAO's winds aloft charts, supplemented by the package of weather data supplied by NOAA and the reports of KE015, we concluded that Chun correctly anticipated a head wind on his actual course very close to the 45-knot head wind we rejected as too strong for R-20. To quote ICAO's summary:

> [The flight plan] wind field was reflected in the winds reported by KE015 which flew along route R20 some ten minutes after KE007. The winds reported by KE007, however, did not reflect [the] forecast wind field and KE007's wind report of 270°/55kt at NEEVA compared with the estimated windflow of 300°/30kt indicated that KE007, reporting NEEVA, was already well to the north of R20.

And:

> The wind report by KE007 at NIPPI, 320°/45kt was also inconsistent with the wind field along R20, such a wind direction being more in keeping with a position at least 200nm north-northwest of NIPPI.[5]

We might also recall the testimony of Captain Park Yong-man of KE015. Park, claiming concern about KE007's nine-minute delay at NEEVA, took the unusual step of contacting Captain Chun directly at about 1603Z. "I asked him, 'What happened, Chun?' He say so there is a so strong wind."[6]

Head winds and wind fields are not stable. They are always shifting as weather patterns change. Nor was KE007's track to Kamchatka an uninterrupted 1,501-mile or 1,429-mile Great Circle course. On the contrary, KE007 made a series of course changes en route to its 1622Z position off the coast, so that the number of miles actually flown was greater than 1,501. And during the flight, KE007's flight crew often had to adjust airspeed above or below 490 knots, and ground speed accordingly, to make good its 1622Z arrival time. Nevertheless, it seems clear to us that in Chun's advance planning a head wind other than that on R-20 did play a key part.

This leaves one further question: If the "ETP" on Chun's flight plan did not stand for "Equal Time Point," what did it stand for?

As we find in the *United States Government Flight Information Publication, Alaska Supplement*, it stood for (and still stands for) something very different.

In the "Civil Procedures" section is a schematic summary of Part 99 of the Federal Aviation Regulations. Part 99 contains operational regulations for civilian aircraft, with specific reference to Domestic Air Defense Identification Zones (ADIZ's). Specifically, aircraft approaching ADIZ's under Visual Flight Rules from without are required to "give ETP at least 15 minutes before penetration."[7]

We make no more of this requirement here than that the obvious meaning of "ETP," and the meaning Captain Chun clearly gave it, is not "Equal Time Point" but "Estimated Time of Penetration." Chun, of course, was using the term not about U.S. domestic airspace but about the airspace into which he was preparing to fly, that of the Soviet Union.

NOTES

1. Or possibly someone else present at the pre-flight briefing. Caj Frostell, head of the ICAO team which conducted the 1993 fact-finding report on the downing, asserts that the handwriting on KE007's flight plan is the same as that on the flight plan of KE007's sister flight, KE015. This gives rise to the possibility that a third party (the dispatcher?) made the notes, presumably contemporaneously, as the flight documentation was impounded by the NTSB nine hours after the downing.

2. Harold H. Ewing, letter to W. R. Johnson, October 8, 1986, p. 2.

3. William A. King, Jr., Flight Information Design Analyst, Jeppesen Sanderson, letter to R. W. Allardyce, January 16, 1987.

4. James Edward Oberg, unpublished essay, "The KAL007 Tragedy: Sense, Nonsense, and Pretense, May 3, 1988," p. 2.

5. *ICAO Report* (1983), p.37

6. *In Re:* Korean Air Lines Disaster of September 1, 1983; *Deposition of Park Yong-man*, p. 70.

7. *United States Government Flight Information Publication, Alaska Supplement*, p. 178.

FLIGHT AND VOICE RECORDERS ADDENDUM

In Chapter 6 of Volume I, we quote a number of Soviet mariners and divers who, interviewed by *Izvestiya*, insisted that the 747's recorders were brought up from beneath the sea in October, 1983, and were locked away for years in some official safe in Moscow. In the Epilogue, we give a brief account of Russian President Boris Yeltsin's dramatic handover of the purported readouts from the black boxes and analyses of their meaning to the members of a U.S. diplomatic delegation; of his later, even more dramatic handover of the purported black boxes themselves to the heads of the South Korean government; and of the ultimate Russian transfer of the purported original black box tapes to representatives of ICAO.

It is worth noting briefly here what so-called "black boxes" are and what data they record. KE007, like all air carrier aircraft, was equipped with two types of recorders. The model 642C-1 Cockpit Voice Recorder (CVR), made by Collins, Inc., retains the last thirty minutes of flight deck discussion and sound on a loop tape. So this would have covered the half-hour prior to the interruption of power. If power had been cut off at 1826.22Z, when Lieutenant-Colonel Gennadiy Osopovich's missiles struck the 747, the final half-hour might have begun as early as 1756Z. This would have been a minute after Osipovich, vectored from Dolinsk out over the Sea of Okhotsk, had begun scanning international airspace for a possible "intruder." In fact, the analysis of the tape prepared by ICAO's consultants in March and April, 1993, places its beginning at 1754.10Z and its ending at 1827.48Z.[1]

The second type of recorder aboard KE007 was a Sundstrand Data Control, Inc. digital flight data recorder

(DFDR), model 573A. The array of flight data recorded directly from sources in the aircraft's instrumentation is impressive. To quote ICAO's list:

> [P]ressure altitude, airspeed, heading, normal acceleration, roll and pitch attitude, longitudinal and lateral acceleration, VHF and HF keying, control column and control wheel positions, rudder pedal position, aileron position, elevator and rudder positions, horizontal stabilizer position, flap handle position, flap position, leading edge flap position, spoiler positions, speed brake handle position, hydraulic pressure, landing gear lever position, squat switch, radio altitude, locator and glide slope deviation, ILS and VOR frequency selection, outer, middle, and inner marker, autopilot engagement, flight director mode, navigation mode switch, speed mode switch, altitude mode switch, auto throttle engagement, stick shaker, ground proximity warning, nacelle temperature, fire warnings, cabin pressure warning, thrust level angle, engine pressure ratio (EPR), reverse thrust and event marker.[2]

A number of these parameters were not recorded on the recovered DFDR: in particular the actual positions of the aircraft's control surfaces (ailerons, elevator and rudder, flaps), of some of its flight deck controls and of its autopilot and INS switches. The recovered recorder itself had suffered damage.[3] Nevertheless, it was possible to draw from the tape a picture of some 27 hours of the Boeing 747's previous flight activity, covering part of a Seoul-Anchorage-New York flight on August 30, 1983, and the return flight from New York to Anchorage, and then across the North Pacific, Kamchatka, the Sea of Okhotsk and Sakhalin to the point of the aircraft's destruction.

Both recorders were located in the fuselage of the aircraft: according to the 1983 *ICAO Report*, they were "above the coat rack in front of the aft left lavatories."[4] The *1993 ICAO Report* placed them "in the Aft Equipment Center . . . in the pressure cabin aft of the left rear passenger door and above the level of the top of the door."[5]

The Digital Flight Data Recorder was equipped with a battery-powered under-water sonar beacon, a "pinger," with a guaranteed battery life of 30 days. Pinger sounds were detected by U.S. search and recovery vessels during the search period. The Soviets assert that some of these, at least, came from a false pinger reportedly deployed by Soviet Admiral Vladimir Vasilyevich Sidorov, then commander of the Pacific Flotilla of the Soviet Navy.

Are the supposed CVR and DFDR black boxes genuine? Are the CVR and DFDR tapes authentic? On the face of it, these questions seem absurd. Under an agreement worked out between the four involved nations: Japan, South Korea, the United States and Russia, the black boxes would be examined and their contents recovered, under ICAO auspices, by the government aviation specialists of a fifth and uninvolved nation, France. "Accordingly, the recovery of information was made by BEA [*Bureau Enquêtes-Accidents*] in Paris. The *Centre d'Essais en Vol* at Brétigny-sur-Orge assisted in the primary recovery of DFDR information."[6] To query the assessments of these experts that the boxes and the tapes are genuine seems foolish in the extreme.

Yet the singular finding that KE007's DFDR, from three minutes after the start of its takeoff until the point of missile impact, recorded a constant magnetic compass flight path of 245°, with no further input by the flight crew, is cause for wonder.

NOTES

1. *1993 ICAO Report*, Background Information, p. 2.

2. *ICAO Report* (1983), p. 28.

3. For a description of the recovered DFDR, its condition and its capabilities, see *1993 ICAO Report*, pp. 28-31.

4. *Loc. cit.*

5. *1993 ICAO Report*, p. 23.

6. *1993 ICAO Report*, p. 22.

TEN-DEGREE ERROR ADDENDUM

In the main body of our work and at greater length in this volume,[1] we discuss various explanations of how KE007 might have "innocently" strayed from its proper J-501/R20 course from Anchorage to Seoul. As we point out in our "Ewing Addendum," perhaps the most widely accepted of these explanations (and certainly the best publicized) is the notion that a member of KE007's flight crew, in preparing the aircraft's computerized Inertial Navigation Systems (INS's) before takeoff at Anchorage, accidentally typed into the memory of the INS that later governed the controls "W139°59.6'" instead of "W149°59.6'" for the longitude of the 747's location at the gate.

According to proponents of this theory, the typing error created a faulty INS "ramp position" ten degrees (289 nautical miles) east of where the aircraft was actually parked. As a result, the longitudes of all of the navigational waypoints along the route to Seoul, though correctly typed, were wrongly sensed. This in turn created a set of "false" waypoints; and in making good its track to these, KE007 increasingly deviated to the north and west of the proper route and eventually and tragically strayed into Soviet airspace.

Based as it is on a type of mistake we all make virtually every day of our lives, this explanation is temptingly plausible. Because we ourselves are forever striking wrong keys on our typewriters or hitting the wrong buttons on our touchtone telephones or miscounting the number of measures of coffee we have put in the pot, it is easy to credit that somebody on KE007's flight deck might have entered a wrong number on an INS keypad -- and that a single wrong number in a super-sensitive navigational device is what led to tragedy.

Nevertheless, a whole host of reasons having to do with both operational practice and navigational and geographic reality makes this version of events impossible to accept. Of these reasons, one of the most elementary is that while a single INS misprogrammed as described above and coupled to the autopilot could have directed the aircraft, the other two Inertial Navigation Systems would have displayed data en route grossly and increasingly at odds with the data displayed by the "command" INS. ICAO, in its report, imagines that an exceptionally inattentive flight crew might not have noticed such discrepancies and puts forward, though without much conviction, the suggestion that the scenario "could be regarded as a possible explanation for KE007's off-track navigation."[2]

But some KE007 investigators, among them Jerald M. Davis, the former senior official of the Federal Aviation Administration who devised the ten-degree error theory, have always been unhappy with the idea that such extreme differences could have been overlooked. They prefer an alternate version: that the longitudinal error was inserted not in one *but in all three* of the Korean airliner's Inertial Navigation Systems.

Apart from the fact that the flight crew would thus not have had to grapple with (and *pari passu* ignore) weirdly conflicting INS readings of times and distances "From" and "To Go" and conflicting waypoint numbers, the concept of a ten-degree error in all three of KE007's INS's is no more respectable than the concept of a ten-degree error in only one. Having dealt with the latter in the "Ewing Addendum" and elsewhere, we feel that for the sake of completeness -- and to lay both versions to rest -- we should also describe and debunk the error-in-all-three scenario.

James Gollin & Robert Allardyce

The theory.
As with the single INS theory, so here: whatever validity it can be given depends in the first instance on a set of unproven, unprovable violations of standard KAL procedures. The first of these is that one member of KE007's flight crew, acting alone, conducted the initialization and programming of the aircraft's INS's on the ground at Anchorage International Airport.

This individual -- so we are meant to believe -- began the initialization process by inputting into the memory of each INS the present or "ramp" location of the aircraft.[3] This should have been N61°10.5'/W149°59.6'; but was instead separately entered in all three INS's as N61°10.5'/W139°59.6'.

Thereafter, the crew member correctly entered in *one* INS the geographical coordinates of a set of waypoints, or discrete locations, along the J-501/R20 air route KE007 was scheduled to fly. The LTN-72R-28 Inertial Navigation System will accept up to nine such waypoints at a time. If a given flight path has more than nine, those beyond the ninth must be entered after the aircraft, in the course of flight, has passed one or more of the first nine.

According to the ten-degree error theorists, the coordinates the crew member inserted were those for:

No.	Waypoint	Latitude/Longitude	Distance (nm)[5]
1	Anc/VOR[4]	N61°09.1'/W150°12.3'	--
2	Cairn Mountain	N61°06.0'/W155°33.0'	162
3	BETHEL	N60°47.1'/W161°49.3'	174
4	NABIE	N59°18.0'/W171°45.4'	312
5	Nukks	N57°15.1'/E179°44.3'	296
6	NEEVA	N54°40.7'/E172°11.8'	297
7	Ninno	N52°21.5'/E165°22.8'	281
8	NIPPI	N49°41.9'/E159°19.3'	279

| 9 | Nytim | N46°11.9′/E153°00.5′ | 330 |
| 10 | NOKKA | N42°23.3′/E147°28.8′ | 330 |

On international air routes like J501/R-20, some waypoints are compulsory reporting points, others non-compulsory. (In the above set of waypoints, the compulsory reporting points are capitalized, the non-compulsory given in capitals and lower-case letters.) As the term suggests, compulsory reporting points are those at which an aircraft's flight crew is required to contact air traffic control by radio and to file "position reports." These must include time of arrival, estimated arrival time at the next waypoint, fuel supply, and wind and temperature conditions. Such reports are not required at non-compulsory reporting points. These "extra" points, while sometimes used for in-flight navigation checks, are not as a rule entered in INS's.

As we shall discover, it is central to the ten-degree error theory that KE007's crew member fed both compulsory and non-compulsory waypoints into the INS's.

Having managed to type the erroneous ramp location separately into each of KE007's INS's, and having entered the correct coordinates of the above course waypoints into one INS, the crew member used this INS's "cross-fill" function to load the course waypoints automatically into the memories of the other two units. All three units then contained the identical (and wrong) navigational data.

At some point after KE007's 1300Z takeoff and 1304.40Z Air Traffic Control clearance to "proceed direct Bethel when able," KE007's flight captain (Chun Byung-In) or copilot (Sohn Dong-Hwin), whichever was flying the aircraft, had to choose the navigational mode by which to operate. On the face of things, the pilot had a number of choices. One alternative was to turn a switch on his INS Mode Selector Unit to "INS." With the Inertial Navigation Unit thus coupled to the autopilot, he could type in on the keypad of the INS Control Display Unit "One to Three." Under ordinary circumstances, this command would have directed the aircraft by gentle degrees onto the Great Circle course (GCc)[6] between the geographic locations of Waypoint One, the Anchorage VOR beacon, and Waypoint Three, the VOR beacon at Bethel, 336nm west of Anchorage.

With the ten-degree error location in their memory banks, however, KE007's INS's sensed that the Anchorage VOR was some 296nm ahead of its actual location -- *and about 282nm ahead of the aircraft's present position.* INS's, like all computer-driven devices, are literal-minded. A command to fly "FROM" Anchorage "TO" Bethel would therefore have made the aircraft reverse course in midflight. It would then indeed have been flying "FROM" Anchorage. And it would have flown eastward -- across Alaska, Canada, the North Atlantic, northern Europe and Asia and the north Pacific -- in meeting the command to fly "TO" Bethel.

This certainly never happened. So whatever method KE007's pilot did use to get his 747 from Anchorage to Bethel, under the ten-degree error theory it could not have been the simple usual method of ordering the INS's to fly the plane from "One to Three." Nor, fascinatingly, could it have been any other method involving control by the INS's. Indeed, when we come to consider the navigational evidence we shall discover that the question of exactly how the aircraft made its way across Alaska is one of the biggest problems confronting adherents of the ten-degree error theory: a question that they must torture reality to answer at all.

For now, let us continue to lay out the theory.

At the point at which KE007's pilot made his choice of navigational modes, the INS's containing the ten-degree error would have computed the distance to Bethel not as 336nm but as some 621nm. Measured from KE007's present position, 621 nautical miles placed "Bethel" at N60°47.1'/W171°49.3' -- a location not on the Alaskan coastline but 282 nautical miles westward out over the Bering Sea.

Here, it is necessary to keep two seemingly unrelated fact in mind.

The first is that KE007's copilot Sohn reported to air traffic control at 1350.09Z that the 747 had passed "real Bethel" at 1349Z and that "I find NABIE at one four three zero."

The second is that NABIE, Waypoint Four on R-20, is 648nm west of Anchorage and only about 86nm south of "false Bethel."

The ten-degree error theorists, knowing both facts, assume (among their many assumptions) that KE007's flight crew had discovered by some means *other than their incorrect INS's* that they were approaching "real Bethel" and that it was time to file a position report. This done, they flew westward under the control of the INS's which by some method as yet undetermined had been programmed to fly them to Waypoint Three, "false Bethel."

At 1435.11Z, copilot Hwang aboard Korean Air Lines flight KE015 told Anchorage Air Traffic control: ". . . [F]orwarding report ah Korean zero zero seven position NABIE one four three two . . . estimating ah NEEVA one five four nine . . ."

In a nutshell, what proponents of the ten-degree error theory insist occurred is that KE007's flight crew, alerted by an INS warning light about two minutes before reaching "false Bethel," Waypoint Three, *assumed that they were reaching real NABIE, Waypoint Four.*

And what happened at "false Bethel" kept on happening all the way across the north Pacific. From "false Bethel," KE007's misprogrammed INS's are supposed to have flown the aircraft to "false NABIE" (N59°18.0'/E1°45.4'), which the crew mistook for real Nukks, Waypoint Five. But the crew filed no position report at "false NABIE," because real Nukks, where it imagined KE007 to be, is a non-compulsory reporting point.

At 1600.46Z, KE015's copilot Hwang again relayed a KE007 position report to Air Traffic Control. ". . . [T]heir position NEEVA one five five eight . . . estimate NIPPI one seven zero eight." In terms of the ten-degree error theory, this must be taken to mean that at 1558Z KE007 had reached "false Nukks," which in its crew's collective mind was real NEEVA, Waypoint Six. But "False Nukks" (N57°15.1'/E169°44.3') is 175.1 nautical miles north of real NEEVA.

The next waypoint on the ten-degree error course was "false NEEVA" (N54°40.7'/E162°11.8'), which the flight crew supposedly thought was real Ninno, Waypoint Seven and another non-compulsory reporting point.

To get from "false NEEVA" to "false Ninno," which the crew -- we are told -- thought was real NIPPI, Waypoint Eight, KE007 all unknowingly traversed the Soviet Kamchatka Peninsula, taking 31 minutes to cover the 225nm of its flight. At 1709.03Z, west of Kamchatka but still within Soviet airspace, KE007's copilot Sohn reported "position ah NIPPI one seven zero seven" and estimated the aircraft's arrival time at NOKKA, the new Waypoint One, as 1826Z.

KE007 never reached NOKKA. Ironically, it was at 1826.22Z that Soviet interceptor pilot Gennadiy Osipovich reported to his ground controller on Soviet Sakhalin Island, 346.4 nautical miles from NOKKA, that his target, KE007, had been destroyed.

Substantiating the theory.

The strongest evidence in support of the ten-degree error theory -- indeed, the only evidence -- is simply that beyond Bethel the distances between waypoints on R20 are roughly the same. (See table on p. 76.) This means that, given fairly constant wind and temperature conditions, the flight times between waypoints could also have been roughly the same. And so, if the very large body of other significant evidence goes unexamined, time and distance data alone do lend some support to the theory that false waypoints ten degrees to the west of their counterparts could have been innocently confused with real waypoints lying on or fairly near the same longitudes. As ICAO's investigators phrased it:

> All succeeding track leg changes [beyond Bethel] 3-4, 4-5, etc., occurred within four minutes of passing abeam the position [sic] where the track changes 4-5, 5-6, etc., should have been made. This was because the leg distances between Bethel and NOKKA all were close to 300nm and comparable to the initial error of 296nm. R20 is also virtually a straight line from Bethel to NOHO and, therefore, there are no significant angular track changes to quickly draw attention to an error. The INS [units] indicated that the aircraft was on course throughout the flight, but there was a large difference between distance and ETAs as displayed by the INS and those shown in the flight plan.[7]

The evidence against the theory.

As noted a few paragraphs earlier, believers in the ten-degree theory must disregard a very large body of evidence. The evidence is of two types, operational and navigational. By itself, the operational evidence with which we begin casts serious doubt on the theory. It is true that the operational evidence by itself cannot *disprove* the theory, simply because no one now living can fully know what KE007's flight crew did or did not do (much less what it thought or felt) during the six hours and more of preflight preparation and actual flight.

It is the navigational evidence to be unfolded after the operational evidence that drives the stake through this theory's heart.

Operational evidence.
The basic premise of the ten-degree error theory -- the tip of the argument, so to speak, on which everything else rests -- is that one member of KE007's flight crew, alone and unsupervised on the flight deck, initialized and programmed all three INS's prior to takeoff. The reasoning behind this premise has to do with the initialization process, which in turn is a function of how the INS's themselves operate.
As we point out elsewhere, INS initialization begins

> [when] electric power is switched on and the latitude/longitude coordinates of the exact spot on which the aircraft is parked are entered via keypad into the memory banks of all INS units.[8]

With this fact in mind, it becomes obvious why the ten-degree error theorists must insist that KE007's INS's were initialized by one crew member acting alone. Consider: this individual would have had to type the ten-degree longitudinal error (139° for 149°) into each of three units, wait each time for the coordinates to appear in the readout and fail to notice each time the disparity between the readout and the coordinates on the Jeppesen ramp diagram. Had any other crew member been present on the flight deck during all of this, he (or they) would inevitably have noticed the triple anomaly and taken corrective action.
In fact, at the time of the KE007 downing Korean Air Lines specifically disallowed INS initialization and programming to be conducted by an unaccompanied crew member. According to

the airline's operations manual:

> F/O [First Officer, copilot] should insert ramp coordinates with reference to the ramp diagram of Jeppesen chart. And then, inserts waypoint coordinates based on flight planning compared with Jeppesen en route chart . . .
> After the completion of pre-flight inspection and INS insertion, all crews [crew members] must confirm INS inserted data in his own station as follows:
> The present position of individual set should be especially confirmed by each crew in accordance with the present position coordinate chart.

Call out	Confirmation		
Coordinates	Capt	F/O	F/E
(Capt.)			
1. waypoint	No. 1	No. 2	No. 3
(9 to 1)[9]			

In other words, while one crew member handles initialization, he does so in the presence of the two other crew members. Then each crew member individually checks the ramp position in his own INS and responds aloud to the captain's reading aloud of the waypoint coordinates.

While rules can be broken, no investigation of which we are aware has uncovered even a scrap of evidence suggesting that KE007's crew violated the above operational procedures -- which are designed, after all, to safeguard the lives of both passengers and crew. Clearly also, unless there had been gross violations the supposed ten-degree error would have been caught while the aircraft was still on the ground.

The next piece of operational evidence involves the set of waypoints the ten-degree error theorists assert the solo crew member inserted in one INS and, via cross-fill, loaded into the two others.

Bear in mind that the ten-degree error theory is bottomed on the assumption that beyond Bethel and out to sea the waypoints in KE007's INS's were all about 300 nautical miles apart. The 296nm westerly dislocation caused by a ten-degree error would have been close enough to 300nm to have led an unalert flight crew to mistake a false Waypoint Three for the true R-20 Waypoint Four, a false Waypoint Four for the true Waypoint Five, and so on. The repeated mismatching would have been masked by the fact that alert light signals and slight changes in course came at more or less appropriate intervals.

But what if the oceanic waypoints KE007's flight crew actually utilized were *not* all more or less 300nm apart?

We indicated above that of the nine waypoints allegedly inserted at Anchorage, four -- Cairn, Nukks, Ninno and Nytim -- are non-compulsory reporting points. We added that these, which fall between compulsory reporting points, are rarely entered in INS's. In point of fact, it was (and is) Korean Air Lines practice not to enter them.

Substantiating that not entering them was the rule at the time of the KE007 downing are the observations of Captain Vernon L. Stone. Stone (now retired) was one of several British Airways supervisor pilots who, under contract to Korean Air Lines, trained the first group of that company's 747 pilots. In conversation with one of us (Allardyce), his comment on waypoint usage was succinct and emphatic: "The fewer the better." Intermediate waypoints are totally unnecessary for navigation. Punching them in only forces insertions of new waypoints earlier during flight and increases the chances of mistake. Accordingly, "We trained the KAL pilots not to use them."[10]

This being the case, KE007's crew, following company regulations, would have entered "the coordinates of the initial approach fix (VOR or NDB) of departure airport . . . into number one waypoint."[11] In other words, Waypoint One would still have been the location of the Anchorage VOR.

The full list of waypoints would thus have been:

No.	Waypoint	Distance
1	ANC/VOR	--
2	BET (Bethel)	336
3	NABIE	312
4	NEEVA	593
5	NIPPI	560
6	NOKKA	660
7	NOHO	163
8	IFH (Inkfish)	117
9	MXT (Matsushima)	101

1	GTC (Niigata)	100

Because Bethel is 336 nautical miles west of Anchorage and NABIE 312 nautical miles west of Bethel, the ten-degree error's 296nm westward displacement of waypoints could still conceivably have allowed the crew to confuse "false Bethel," Waypoint Two in this sequence with real NABIE, Waypoint Three.

Thus, Copilot Sohn, as his INS alert light blinked on for the first time during the flight to signal that the aircraft was approaching "false Bethel" -- the approach to *real* Bethel had supposedly manifested itself, as we shall see, by other means -- would have started putting together a position report. Either not noticing or wilfully ignoring that the "FROM" waypoint on his Control Display Unit readout was "1" (ANC/VOR) and the "TO" readout "2," (false Bethel), Sohn would have believed the 747 to be nearing NABIE (actually, of course, false NABIE), Waypoint Three.

To come up with the mandatory estimated time of arrival (ETA) at KE007's next waypoint, false NEEVA (Waypoint Four), Sohn would have turned his Control Display Unit master switch to DIS/TIME to quiz his INS. Even though the aircraft was nearing Waypoint Two, not Waypoint Three, the ten-degree error proponents insist that Sohn typed in "3" to "4." This would have given him time and distance figures from false NABIE to false NEEVA -- about seventy-five minutes and 600 nautical miles -- and these were close enough to the real NABIE-real NEEVA figures not to cause him any alarm.[12]

A few miles shy of false Bethel, the INS-autopilot complex "leg-switched" KE007 gently onto the next segment of its journey. Sohn would have relaxed in his seat, confident that he had an hour and a quarter and 600nm in hand before his next position report.

But beyond this, the ten-degree error argument runs no farther -- because KE007, after this leg-switch, would have been traversing not Sohn's imagined 600nm between false NABIE and false NEEVA but rather the 326nm between false Bethel and false NABIE.

So in only forty minutes instead of the expected seventy-five, Sohn's alert light would have flashed on (as would those of his fellow crew members) to signal an approaching waypoint. And two minutes after this, a turn of five degrees to the south would have placed the aircraft on another new heading.

But even if we suppose with the ten-degree error theorists

that Sohn and his mates had missed these cues, other anomalies would soon have presented themselves. Thirty-five minutes later, when in Sohn's mind KE007 would have been reaching NEEVA -- on the ten-degree error flight path, false NEEVA -- *no* alert light would blink and no heading change would take place, because the INS's would still be sensing false NEEVA as another thirty minutes and 240 nautical miles further west than Sohn imagined it to be.

How these freakish happenings could have failed to arouse KE007's crew is not an easy question to answer. The only answer, indeed, is to imagine that the crew was using non-compulsory as well as compulsory reporting points as INS waypoints.[13] But why would a flight crew innocently intent on flying from Anchorage to Seoul violate company policy in this way? Beyond a naked assertion, the ten-degree error scenarists offer no evidence that it happened -- that any but the usual waypoints were used. As for the crew's motivation, they supply none.

A third piece of operational evidence has to do with the use KE007's crew made of the computerized flight plan for the flight.

It has been suggested that the crew, although faithfully consulting their INS's for such data as spot winds and temperatures, either failed to check or disbelieved their INS readouts of waypoint numbers, waypoint latitude/longitude positions and times and distances "TO" and "FROM" waypoints. Other than the INS's, the only source of this information, essential for position reports and ETA's, was the flight plan. So ten-degree error enthusiasts sometimes theorize that the crew simply read its arrival-time estimates directly from the flight plan.

To accept this notion, one must overlook that, as ICAO investigators put it, "KE007's position reports did not coincide exactly with its flight plan estimates."[14]

One must also overlook an operating practice universal in commercial aviation. INS's refer to waypoints by number, while crew members and air traffic controllers refer to them by name. To rule out any possibility of confusion, during preflight briefings crew members habitually write the INS numbers of the waypoints beside the names on their copies of the flight plan. So if KE007's crew did get the numbers mixed up *a là* the ten-degree error theory, all three members must have been ignoring both their INS's and their flight plans throughout the entire course of the tragic flight.

Navigational evidence.

Whatever one makes of the operational evidence against the ten-degree error theory, the navigational evidence against it is crushing.

The simplest way to put forward this evidence is to start with the first leg of KE007's flight, the leg that took it from Anchorage westward over Alaska and past Bethel. As we point out in our analysis, radars located at Kenai and King Salmon Air Forces Bases tracked KE007 for virtually all of this portion of the flight. Analysis of the radar returns (which were certified for accuracy by the FAA divisional superintendent at Anchorage) proves that KE007, starting at 1309.05Z, was being controlled by its INS's and, at 1312.11Z, was directed onto a Great Circle course. This GCc, too smooth according to the radar returns to have been flown manually, carried the 747 westward, but not directly over the Bethel waypoint. Instead, it took KE007 some 12.6nm north of the Bethel VOR.[15]

In December, 1983, the ICAO investigating team used a Boeing Aviation flight crew training simulator and Litton Aero Products INS's to test various "innocently lost" theories, including the ten-degree error theory. One of its findings, subsequently tested and retested by us, was simply that KE007, whether the ten-degree error was in one or in all three INS's, would have *"passed much further north of Bethel than did the actual flight (38nm versus 12nm)."*[16] [Emphasis added.]

In a word, *KE007's actual track over Alaska as verified by radar and the ten-degree error track are not the same and cannot possibly be reconciled.*

Furthermore, had the aircraft's INS's sensed that Bethel was 296nm further west than it really was, no two-minute alert light would have blinked on as KE007 approached the real Bethel to signal that a waypoint was coming up. And yet, copilot Sohn reported reaching Bethel at "four-niner," 1349Z -- about when KE007 would have done so on a normal flight.

Ten-degree error apologists have come up with a bizarre explanation of both these fundamental flaws in their theory. Namely, that despite the incontrovertible radar evidence to the contrary, KE007 was not on a Great Circle course at all over Alaska! Instead, they say, it was being flown, either by hand or autopilot, on a magnetic course.[17] The idea was to aim the aircraft via its compasses in the general direction of Bethel and, once within range of the Bethel VOR, to home in on this powerful radio beacon with its reach of over 200 nautical miles. The reason KE007 passed 12.6nm north of the VOR instead of directly over it was that a southerly cross wind unnoticed (and uncompensated for) by the crew blew the 747 north. And the reason that co-pilot Sohn Eui-Dong knew to contact Anchorage at the right time was because he saw the needles on the dials of the VOR indicators, which function independent of the INS, flick sharply to the left as the aircraft passed abeam of the Bethel VOR.[18]

Apart from what the radar returns prove, the winds that night would have blown KE007 south, not north, of a magnetic course track toward the Bethel VOR.

If, however, we toss out the radar and meteorological evidence and swallow for the sake of the argument that KE007 did fly toward Bethel on a magnetic course but somehow bypassed it, we must wonder what the aircraft and its crew did next. One answer put forward by the ten-degree error theorists is that beyond Bethel the pilot flicked the switch of his autopilot from "HDG" to "INS," and that the autopilot, now under the control of its INS's, then guided the aircraft gently onto the ten-degree error course.

But this could not have happened. An aircraft's Inertial Navigation Systems can only capture a "desired track" -- i. e., the track of which the waypoints are in their memories -- *if the track is less than seven nautical miles distant.*

When KE007 passed Bethel, it was some 25.4nm south of the ten-degree error point of passage. Had Captain Chun or copilot Sohn merely turned the autopilot switch to "INS," nothing would have happened. KE007 would have continued flying out to sea, its direction dictated for the moment by the last compass heading fed into its autopilot. *And it never would have flown close enough to the ten-degree error track to join it.*[19]

An alternative answer is that, once past Bethel, the pilot in command turned the autopilot switch to "INS" and then typed in "Zero" to "Three." As noted above, "Zero" is always the present position of the aircraft. So this command would immediately have turned KE007 onto the GCc from its present position to "false Bethel." For this to have happened, Chun and Sohn, in their innocence, would have to have overlooked that Sohn had just reported passing Waypoint Three. They would also have to have ignored that their aircraft had made a northward turn of at least eight degrees (the further past Bethel the 747's position at the time of switching to INS, the more acute the turn) instead of the anticipated five-degree southward turn normal at Bethel on R-20. They would have to have taken

positive action, which wipes out the ten-degree error theorists'
hypothesis of a completely passive flight crew.

Even more of a barrier to credibility is the issue of the
aircraft's putative speed.

At 1350.14Z, we recall, copilot Sohn reported reaching
Bethel at 1349Z and estimated KE007's time of arrival at
NABIE as 1430Z, allowing forty-one minutes for this leg of the
747's journey. At 1349Z, as the aircraft was passing 12.6nm
north of Bethel, "false Bethel," which we are told the crew later
confused with NABIE, was 292.7nm away. To cover 292.7
nautical miles in forty-one minutes calls for a groundspeed of
428 knots. As he passed abeam Bethel, Sohn reported a
21-knot head wind (295 degrees at 25k) and an outside air
temperature (OAT) of minus 49C. Had KE007 actually flown
to "false Bethel "from abeam real Bethel, its True Air Speed
would have been 449 knots, or an astonishingly slow and
completely illicit M.767!

Despite all of these glaring unlikelihoods, the "Zero" to
"Three" proposition at least offers a technically possible means
of getting KE007 -- somehow and somewhere -- onto the
ten-degree error track. Accordingly, let us accept it for the
moment and follow the aircraft as it crossed the Bering Sea
toward Soviet Kamchatka.

A minor but intriguing sidelight is shed by the testimony of
USAF Air Surveillance Officer Captain Michael E. Valentine
in the civil liability lawsuit brought by the families of KE007
victims. Captain Valentine was one of the "trackers" on duty in
the NORAD Regional Operations Control Center (ROCC) at
Elmendorf Air Force Base in Anchorage on August 31, 1983.
His task was to follow on ROCC radar the tracks of aircraft in
the Alaskan Distant Early Warning Identification Zone
(DEWIZ).[20] In the course of his testimony, Captain Valentine
testified that KE007, had it penetrated the Alaskan Buffer Zone

at all, would have remained within it for such a short period that it would have been impossible for ROCC trackers to spot it and warn it via the FAA that it was heading into danger. In fact, on the supposed ten-degree error track KE007 would have entered the Buffer Zone at N60°29.5′/W173°40.0′ on an instant heading of 257.2°. It would have exited the Buffer Zone at N59°36.5′/W180°00.0′. The distance covered during the penetration would have been 196.9nm. Based on the figures given in copilot Sohn's 1444.20Z update, KE007, flying at M.876, would have remained in the off-limits area for 26.5 minutes! Whatever Captain Valentine told the court, this would have afforded ROCC ample time to reach civilian air traffic controllers who in turn could have forwarded a warning.[21]

To return to the navigational evidence, the ICAO simulations cited above indicate that an innocently off-course KE007 plugging along the ten-degree error track at M.840 would have reached "false Nukks" (N57°15.1′/E169°44.3′) at 1550Z.[22]

But one minute later, at 1551Z, the Soviets say they spotted KE007 on radar at a location we have pinpointed as N58°24.8′/E167°17.3′.[23] The U.S., which monitored virtually all Soviet tracking of KE007, has confirmed the time. In 1992, the Central Intelligence Agency declassified and released to us a new set of coordinates of KE007's 1551Z location: N58°03.0′/E170°15.0′.[24] This location is some 77.6nm east of the Soviet location. In 1993, the ICAO investigative team secured a list of radar fixes and their coordinates as "read" by U.S. intelligence from Soviet radar and certified by Russian sources as accurate. This gives KE007's 1551Z position as N58°03.0′/E169°45.0′, some 15.9nm further east and thus somewhat closer to the Soviet location.

Whichever position is the correct one, the distances between "false Nukks" on the ten-degree error track and each of them are such that under the laws of physics, there is no way that KE007 could have covered them in one minute flat.

The ten-degree error theorists solve this problem handily: they ignore the Soviet and U.S. radar fixes entirely.

They do of course insist that KE007 reached "false Nukks," albeit they suppose it did so considerably later than the 1550Z which would have been reasonable, according to ICAO, given KE007's weight, speed and altitude and the wind and weather conditions along the ten-degree error track.

Under the ten-degree error theory, KE007's crew mistook "false Nukks" for real NEEVA. In the position report for KE007 relayed at 1600.46Z, KE015 told air traffic control: ". . . their position at NEEVA one five five eight." This 1558Z arrival time was really, so the theorists must believe, KE007's time of arrival at "false Nukks." The supposition gives rise to yet another interesting set of times and distances. Thus, the State Department's chronology of the flight gives 1635Z as the time when the "airliner enters over Kamchatka landmass."[25]

If the point of entry on the ten-degree error course was N53°58.4'/E159°55.0', about 10nm south of Zhuposovo, then the distance between "false Nukks" and the point of entry is 386.1 nautical miles. The ten-degree error theorists tell us that KE007 covered this distance in thirty-seven minutes (between 1558Z and 1635Z). This meant a ground speed of 626 knots. KE007's relayed report made mention of a 49-knot head wind, which made KE007's True Air Speed 675 knots, which translates into M1.13! No matter what the error theorists say, the 747 does not fly at 113 per cent of the speed of sound.

Another possibility must be taken into account. An aircraft on the ten-degree error track would just graze the tip of Cape Kronitskiy on its way southwestward across Kronitskiy Bay, entering over the main part of the peninsula at the fix given just above. If the tip of Cape Kronitskiy (N54°34.0'/E161°48.0') was the State Department's 1635Z point of entry, the distance to be covered between "false Nukks" and the "Kamchatkan landmass" is 311 nautical miles, not 386.1. This lowers KE007's ground speed to 504 knots, its True Air Speed to 553 knots and its Mach number to a "mere" M.947, also an impossible speed for a 747.

And so, we come to the final fact of navigational evidence. Had KE007 flown the track mandated by the ten-degree error theory, it would have entered over Kamchatka some 30 or 40 nautical miles south (depending on which of the above entry-points one selects) of the point of actual entry as shown on Soviet radar and confirmed to within 600 feet by the U.S. Furthermore, the point of exit on the ten-degree error track is some eight nautical miles south of the actual point of exit.

As over Alaska, then, so over Kamchatka: the ten-degree error course cannot be made to overlie KE007's actual flight path.

The discrepancy, indeed, is significant enough to have caused Jerald M. Davis, the *originator* of the ten-degree error theory, after eight years, to cast doubt on his own theory -- to decide to "check to see if maybe the error wasn't bigger than ten degrees -- maybe ten and a half degrees."[26] When the ten-and-a-half-degree error scenario was disproved by navigational analysis, Davis offered no fewer than five additional misprogrammings of KE007's initial position on the ramp at Anchorage.[27] Further analysis of each, in terms of the resulting waypoints, speeds, times, locations and fuel usages, demonstrated conclusively that these new models fit the facts no better than does the original.

Conclusions.
    The most striking feature of the ten-degree error theory is its superficiality. Neither its originator nor the many

investigators, journalists, lawyers and propagandists who have adopted the theory in one or the other of its two forms seem ever to have looked seriously at the mass of evidence which contradicts it. It has been argued that much of this evidence was unavailable at the time the theory was developed (September to mid-November, 1983). In fact, the single most important piece of evidence, the FAA-certified radar returns of KE007's flight across Alaska, was available and was used by ICAO in its 1983 report to discredit the version of the theory which had the error in all three inertial navigation systems.

By January, 1984, in any event, the flight and radio communications data that enabled us to determine KE007's real flight path, speeds and distances covered had been released. So too had the Soviet data, suspect as these were. Although other material (e.g., the JSDA radar returns, the deposition of KE015's Captain Park Yong-Man, the readouts from the Cockpit Voice Recorder and Digitalized Flight Data Recorder) did not become available until much later, an abundance of negative evidence was accessible to investigators.

Nevertheless, the ten-degree error theory soon became the canonical account of why KE007 flew where it did fly.

Perhaps the most important reason for the theory's wide acceptance was its espousal by writer Seymour Hersh. Hersh, considered an outstanding investigative journalist, centered the last third of his book on KE007, "*The Target Is Destroyed*", on the in-one-INS version of the theory as interpreted by Flying Tiger pilot Harold H. Ewing.[28]

Even more sanction was given to the ten-degree error theory when the Plaintiffs' Steering Committee, the cadre of liability lawyers representing the families of those killed in the downing, made it the linchpin of their multi-million-dollar lawsuit against Korean Air Lines.

The reason the ten-degree error theory appeals to the

lawyers is that it is essentially non-controversial. It heaps guilt on KE007's flight crew, first for committing the error and failing to catch it, later for "willful misconduct" in continuing to fly in dangerous skies even though crew members knew their INS's were malfunctioning. It places the financial burden of liability squarely on Korean Air Lines and its insurance carriers, entirely relieving the U.S. government of any liability. It pleases the trial judge in the case, Judge Aubrey E. Robinson of the Federal District Court in Washington, D.C., who has from the outset resisted on grounds of national security any effort to implicate the government. Until 1991, it even pleased the attorneys for Korean Air Lines, because they felt it based the case against their client rather narrowly on the 1983 *ICAO Report*, which they thought the U.S. Supreme court might exclude on evidentiary grounds.

Yet, for all of this popularity, it is crystal-clear that the ten-degree error theory (and its many cousins) was shallow and biased. It was first and foremost an apologia for the "innocently lost" view of the KE007 excursion. As we have pointed out at painful length, it is concocted almost entirely of conjecture about what a supremely incompetent, vegetable flight crew might or might not have done. At the same time, it carefully overlooked an enormous body of indisputable factual evidence about what the aircraft and its crew actually did do.

NOTES

1. See Vol. I, pp. 9-10; 18-21; and Vol. II, pp. 10-12.

2. *ICAO Report* (1983), p. 52.

3. In navigation by INS, the present or instant position of the aircraft is always "Position Zero."

4. "Anc/VOR" stands for the Anchorage Very High Frequency Omni Range beacon, a key navigational aid located on Fire Island, some seven nautical miles west and slightly south of Anchorage International Airport.

5. Distances are distances between waypoints, not cumulative distances from Anchorage, in nautical miles.

6. For explanations of the term "Great Circle course," see Vol. I, p. 18, endnote 5; Vol. II, pp. 10-18.

7. *ICAO Report* (1983), p. 49.

8. Vol. II, "Inertial Navigation Systems Addendum," p. 25.

9. "Korean Air Lines B747 Operations Manual," August 1, 1981, p. 04.40.07, in *ICAO Report* (1983), Attachment B, p. 21.

10. Sugwong Kang, a South Korean academician, has told one of us (Allardyce) that Korean Air Lines pilots he has interviewed confirm that company practice is to use only mandatory reporting-points as INS waypoints. Caj E. Frostell, senior ICAO official active in preparing the 1983 *ICAO Report* and head of the team which produced the 1993 report, disagrees. "We were told the opposite by KAL." He notes that all reporting points were listed in the flight log (which is not the same as the INS) and that "the crew on the KAL flight from Anchorage to Seoul on which I travelled on 3 Oct 1983, entered all the reporting points . . . into the INS." Frostell to Richard Witkin, enclosure in letter *c*. November, 1991. Frostell seems not to admit the possibility that his presence prompted the KAL crew to add the non-compulsory reporting points.

11. "Korean Air Lines B747 Operations Manual," p. 04.40.07.

12. Son could have typed in "Zero to Four" for the time and distance from KE007's present position to false NEEVA, but with the ten-degree error in the INS's the figures would have been an alarming one hundred twelve minutes and 900 or so nautical miles. So ten-degree error proponents necessarily rule out this alternative.

13. The non-compulsory reporting point Nukks *is* some forty minutes and 300 nautical miles west of false NABIE. If the crew had inserted false Nukks as one waypoint, the blinking of an alert light forty minutes after passage of what was supposedly NABIE would have come as no surprise.

14. *ICAO Report* (1983), p. 52. Thus, KE007's flight plan showed an ETA at NABIE of 1433Z, but the NABIE ETA copilot Son reported at abeam Bethel was 1430Z; its flight plan NEEVA ETA was 1550Z, but its en route NEEVA ETA (relayed by KE015) was 1549Z; its flight plan NIPPI ETA was 1701Z, its en route NIPPI ETA (also relayed by KE015) was 1708Z; its flight plan NOKKA ETA was 1820Z, its en route NOKKA ETA, 1826Z.

15. Vol. I, pp. 15-21 and, for our detailed analysis of the returns, Vol. II, pp. 13-18.

16. *ICAO Report* (1983), p. 52.

17. As well as needing to overcome the discrepancy between the ten-degree error INS track and KE007's real track, the apologists sorely need some way of flying the plane that kept everybody's eyes steadily off the INS's. Even one stolen glance a minute after takeoff would have led to furious action on the flight deck: the distance "FROM" 1 (the Anchorage VOR) to 3 (in ten-degree error theory lore the Bethel VOR), instead of showing up as about 330nm, would have been over 600 nm.

18. If Son had really been watching his dials this closely, he would have had great difficulty *not* noting that the bar on the adjacent Horizontal Situation Indicator had floated so far to the right side of the indicator dial that it was almost out of sight, revealing that KE007, though 12.6nm north of Bethel, was far south of the track in its INS's, that being the track of the ten-degree error course. Any seasoned pilot, seeing such a displacement, would have reacted instantly.

19. For the record: According to the last radar returns KE007 would have flown seaward on an instant magnetic heading of 249.8°. But a wind of 25 knots blowing at an angle of 295° would have produced a southward drift of 3°. With its autopilot switch in "INS" position but no desired track within joining distance and no further instructions input into the INS's, KE007 would have drifted further and further southward of the ten-degree error track and would in fact have passed well to the south of Kamchatka. We note also that under these circumstances KE007 would have been well within range of the Air Traffic Control relay station on St. Paul Island and could have radioed its NABIE position report directly to Anchorage. (See Vol. I, pp. 34, 38.)

20. *In re*: Korean Air Lines Disaster of September 1, 1983, "Statement of Genuine Issues of Material Fact and Plaintiffs' Steering Committee's Opposition to the Government's Motion for Summary Judgment,"

August 30, 1985, pp. 27-29.

21. This is equally true with respect to the course KE007 actually did fly through the Buffer Zone. See Vol. I, pp. 42-46.

22. *ICAO Report* (1983), p. 51. The position given in the report (2.14.8.4) is the position where leg-switching would have taken place. We use the actual position of false Nukks, a few nautical miles to the west.

23. We take this fix from the map the Soviet State Commission for Civil Aviation Flight Safety in the USSR supplied ICAO. See *ICAO Report* (1983), p. F-17; Vol. I, p. 53.

24. See Vol. I, pp. 52-53 and *passim*.

25. U.S. State Department telegram 83 State 254088.

26. Jerald M. Davis, conversation with Richard Witkin, November 8, 1991.

27. For the record, these required KE007's flight crew to mistake KE007's Anchorage position by: E11°0.7' (plus a latitude displacement of N9.9°); E11°15.0'; E11°43.7'; E11°52.7'; E12° (plus a latitude displacement of N00°20.0'). Obviously, none of these errors could have been produced by punching in one wrong number.

28. For our analysis of Ewing's theorizing, see Vol. II, pp. 33-50. "Ewing Addendum."